ONE DISH - FOUR SEASONS

ONE DISH – FOUR SEASONS

Food, Wine, and Sound – All Year Round

By Jordan Zucker

Recipes by Jordan Zucker and Betti Zucker

Wines by Jordan Zucker and Jim Zucker

DEDICATION

For all of the mothers who enable dreams, daughters who execute dreams, and fathers who support dreams. Sometimes it takes a village. Sometimes it just takes a family.

ISBN-13: 978-0-692-16720-5

First Edition: October 2019

Design by: Signé Higgins
Illustrations by: Dan Skurow
Photographs by: Pete Lee
Food Styling by: Vivian Lui
Pre-press by: Chris Shadrick and Ben Kautt

Packaged by Rock Out Books
P.O. Box 460054
San Francisco, CA 94146
Email: info@rockoutbooks.com

Printed in China

Introduction

HELLO, I'M JORDAN AND MY FOLKS ARE BETTI AND JIM.
Meet the Zuckers. We are a food family. We live to eat, in spite of the scientific evidence that we do the reverse, eat to live. Dining has always been warm and welcoming in my family. It's inclusive. It's celebratory. In fact, we cherish every opportunity to throw a dinner party, from impromptu summer barbecues to Rosh (Hashanah) dinners to Thanks-g., the Super Bowl, and even the dog's "Bark Mitzvah." At my high school reunion, my classmates were still reminiscing

about the tantalizing aromas that filled our house, because my mother was always cooking something badass and fancy.

We also live to drink, especially wine. Ever since I can remember, I've been allowed a sip of whatever my folks were drinking. We're American, but we get out a lot. As with many bon vivants, my folks resonated particularly with the French culture; they served salad last and the children were allowed to taste the wine. (The children were also required to sit through a ballet.) My parents spoke French in front of me at the dinner table when they didn't want me to understand what they were saying, and then later conveniently insisted I learn Spanish in school because it was "more practical." One night when I was about 7 years old, we were dining at The Inn at Sawmill Farm, the only jacket-and-tie restaurant in the Deerfield Valley, where our Vermont country home was located. My dad had just been teaching me how to hold a glass of wine up to a light and estimate its age based on the color (purple edges, younger; brown edges, older). When the sommelier opened the bottle and offered a taste to my dad, he deferred to little me: "Jordan, what vintage do you think this bottle is?" I held the glass up to the dim light. The wine clearly was much older than I was. "It's a 1970!" I proclaimed, nailing it exactly. The sommelier refused to return to our table—to this day, one of Jim's proudest moments. Everyone's favorite room in the Vermont house is the wine cellar, air conditioned to a regulation 55 degrees, with a 5-inch-thick arched wooden door and an old-school padlock and key that looks like it was swiped from the set of *Game of Thrones*.

And because a proper indulgent life isn't complete without ambiance, we are also a music family. My parents took me to the Simon & Garfunkel concert in Central Park when I was a little girl—or a baby if I'm going to maintain my age ruse. Even today we're constantly singing and harmonizing to the soundtrack to our lives. For me, the music really gets rolling while I'm preparing and cooking a meal. Maybe I chop to the beat. Maybe I sing to the tomatoes. Maybe I dance around the kitchen while my dog stares at me, deciding if she should be embarrassed, confused, or enamored. Music sets the mood. It's as universally connective a tissue as food is for defining a culture or generation. It's a source of bonding, whether you're at a concert venue or dining table. It carries the picture of the season, time of day, tone of mood, base of emotion. I bet you unconsciously pair music with your food rather often. And if you don't, give it a whirl!

I tend to narrate my day through song, which is super endearing and never annoying to my friends and neighboring strangers. For example, when someone comes to pick me up, I'm likely to bust out a "Grab your things, I've come to take you home..." from Peter Gabriel's "Solsbury Hill." Come to think of it, most of our family stories and memories are centered around meals, cocktails, and music. With those three elements—food, wine, and music—squared away, you're pretty much guaranteed a successful and joyful meal, conducted in English, French, or any other language with which you're expressing yourself.

"They had a hi-fi phono, boy, did they let it blast
Seven hundred little records, all rock, rhythm and jazz
But when the sun went down, the rapid tempo of the music fell
"C'est la vie," said the old folks, it goes to show you never can tell"
— Chuck Berry, "You Never Can Tell"

Cut to six years ago, maybe more—we definitely didn't churn this thing out overnight. My mother wanted to create a cookbook that would examine the evolution of individual dishes throughout the course of the year. Most seasonal cookbooks are divided into winter, spring, summer, and fall sections that include a list of ingredients harvested during each season, along with fabulous recipes that showcase the ingredients from each separate list. We decided to take a different angle and go in reverse. Instead of having a shopping list of seasonal ingredients to launch you, we take what you're in the mood for—a salad, a pasta, a meatball, a dip—and show you how to update each one for each season, based on which items look most appealing at your local market at any moment. Whether it serves as hand-holding, training wheels, or just a pep talk, this book should give you the confidence and inspiration to improvise in the kitchen using peak ingredients all year round.

This approach stems from our core philosophy of eating fresh and sourcing local produce. Cooking from scratch is how we roll. The benefits of "seasonizing" (my new term for seasoning per season) include farm-to-table nutrition, local economy support, and satisfying your body's need for specific nutrients at different times of the year sourced from naturally coordinated plant harvest times, which is a highly unscientific theory I just made up. But seriously, using fresh, seasonal vegetables and avoiding products that have been shipped long distances supports what I think are the two most important factors in cooking: **flavor and nutrition**. Produce that gets shipped must be harvested before it's ripe and sometimes may even be frozen. This lengthens its shelf life, but sacrifices its vitamin and flavor concentration. (see "Quality of Ingredients" on page 11). With the increasing popularity of farmers' markets in many cities, there are more opportunities to eat like a locavore.

Once our recipes were established, I decided to complete the aforementioned "entertaining trifecta" by pairing each dish with a wine and a music album. My mother, Betti with an "i," is an artist. My dad, Jim (or as my adorable Bulgarian thick-accented maternal grandmother, Gracie, called him, "Jems"), is an intellectual. This dichotomy usually ensures an entertaining dynamic. I round out the family trio with a somewhat valiant attempt at straddling the left and right brain. Thus, we are applying our Betti-Jim-Jordan Zucker trifecta stamp onto a food-wine-music recipe trifecta book.

Once properly equipped with our roadmap, we set off on an odyssey of writing and cooking, testing and rewriting, a little fighting because that's the normal family dynamic, but also celebrating and eating and collaborating away. We shelved the project for some periods of time. We dusted it off. We reexamined it. We rewrote, re-tested, re-paired. We shopped. We platformed. We photographed. We designed. We missed deadlines and hit roadblocks. We kept forging ahead. And here we are today. We proudly present to you our book, *One Dish—Four Seasons, Food Wine and Sound — All Year Round*.

"Winter, Spring, Summer, or Fall
All you have to do is call
And I'll be there, yes I will
You've got a friend"
– In the produce aisle of the market and in the Zucker family.
– Carole King, "You've Got a Friend"

How to Use This Book

One Dish—Four Seasons takes 20 everyday base recipes and churns out a winter, spring, summer, and fall version of each created by varying a few readily accessible ingredients. In all, we make 20 dishes x 4 seasons = 80 dishes + 1 cocktail x 4 = 84 recipes.

For example, we are not showing you four ways to make a chicken pot pie. If we were to have a pot pie, there would be four variations of it and one season would include chicken. (Is that a sequel I smell?)

Each dish (all 84 of them!) also gets paired with a wine and a music album. To me, these are the three pillars of entertaining that embody a vibe driven by each season.
Food + Wine + Music. They're kind of my religion.

Winter will warm you, but also invigorate like a bright, crisp blue sky after a snowfall.
Spring will awaken you, budding new sensory memories.
Summer will rock you, sweaty heat and ocean breezes.
Fall with hold you, woody and spicy and colorful.

T or F: I used to write for *Hustler*. (F)

One Dish—Four Seasons is color coded with lots of visual aids to illustrate which season you're in and how each recipe varies throughout the year (base recipe in black text; seasonal variations in color). The fundamental point is to start with a base recipe, source locally, and create something healthful and delicious based on your findings at the market on any given day—along with memorable get-togethers that will bloom in any season.

So here it is—I threw it all out on the dining-room table like a Rummikub board.
The hook: The pairings. The seasonal good-time recipe trifecta.
And away we go.

A NOTE ON EXPERIMENTATION:

This book was designed to impart a little education and a dash of confidence in the kitchen, showing you how to treat a basic recipe as a canvas and modify it to suit your tastes, mood, and readily available seasonal market ingredients. A recipe in general is a guide. Use ours strictly, or merely as inspiration for your own versions and visions. Though it's dependable enough to reference for a recipe on any given day, it's meant to be didactic. Master the process and turn it into your own. Have fun, be creative, make mistakes, discover happy accidents. The lesson is sometimes the reward.

A NOTE ON SEASONALITY:

When I had friends over to test the recipes, they asked how strictly the seasons should be followed, "because I want this one all the time!" (See page 56, summer guac.) Yes. Fine. Importing and trade may enable certain seasonal ingredients to be stocked and available during off-season months. So you *can* make a broccoli soup in the summer and a pea soup in the fall if you can find lovely components to satisfy such rebellious cravings, but as previously mentioned, their nutrition and flavor concentration will likely have taken a hit. We advocate locally sourced and freshly harvested ingredients as much and whenever possible. Go with what looks the best at the market.

As for the pairings, I picked wines and music that I like in general. Then I explored which pairings worked together to optimize harmony of each season, course, and dish. There are also a few extra layers on top of that, with plays on words, puns, and other cerebral matches. The concept of seasonality functions as a subtle mood informer. I'm a rule breaker and will drink red with fish and white with meat. While the heavier selections here tend to dominate the colder months, there's no reason you *can't* go big in the summer or chilled in the winter. I'm just encouraging a present vibe creation for each season.

And now, a few basic housekeeping rules we treat as gospel in the Zucker kitchen.

QUALITY OF INGREDIENTS:

I've seen people take shortcuts in recipes and then wonder why the recreated dish didn't come out as well as the original. Quality of ingredients plays a huge role in final dish outcome. Your dish is only as good as its elements. Sure, it helps to know which flavors pair well and how to properly season and combine, but a tried-and-true recipe will never shine without proper quality ingredients. Be picky with your produce. Have pride in your prime cuts. I often go to the market with a rough sketch of what I want to make, and then finalize the menu based on what looks good when I get there. That's the underlying philosophy that fuels this book. It should help guide you to create masterpieces based on what looks the freshest and most appealing selection on any given day at the market. A bland tomato will never shine even if it's doused in a decadent sauce or hidden, buried deep in a salad. Each ingredient has a significant role, even if it isn't the obvious star of the dish.

While we may dine all fancy-shmancy and appreciate sophisticated flair in the kitchen, that's not what we practice at home. All of our stuff is approachable and surmountable. The ingredients are the fancy part, not the twelve-person kitchen assembly line.

SWOOP

season with olive oil pepper

Seasoning Rule #1:
SWOOPS! SWOOPS! SWOOPS!

Our cardinal rule, universal step, key ingrained requisite practice: SWOOPS! Season with Olive Oil, Pepper and Salt.

Make it your mantra until it becomes second nature in the kitchen. These are the basic essential staples of any kitchen.

But not just any salt, pepper, and olive oil. Make sure they're high quality.
Salt should be coarse, and kept readily available in a little bowl or dish, so you can add your pinches liberally. Salt from a shaker is shunned. You don't know this, but many people are silently judging you when you sprinkle table salt from a shaker.
Pepper should be freshly ground. Crack fresh peppercorns with a grinder instead of using dried shaker pepper. It makes a world of difference. Sing the Byrds' classic with every turn of the pepper grinder: "For every season, Turn, Turn, Turn."
And the **olive oil** should always be flavorful. There are many high-quality options that don't break the bank. Go out and taste them!

We found ourselves SWOOPSing away so much that we came up with our own acronym for it. There's not much I'd cook, serve, or eat without SWOOPSing first. I even SWOOPS individual ingredients along the way before mixing them all together. The trick is finding the right balance of how much. Hint: More than you think. When I say add salt, I'm not messing around. Proper SWOOPSing will make or break your kitchen style. But SWOOPS to your own taste levels. A recipe may suggest exact measurements of olive oil, pepper, and salt, but when it comes down to it, the food should have a light coating of all three. Even SWOOPS things you wouldn't think to, e.g., fruit! It'll get you everywhere. It is the minimum work required to turn any worthy ingredient into a notable opus.

SWOOPS, there it is! — Tag Team (ish)

"More more more.
How do you like it, how do you like it?
More more more!"
— *Andrea True Connection,*
"More, More, More"

Herb Blurb

Fresh herbs are vital to seasonal cooking. Dried spices have their own roll, but certainly not as a replacement for fresh herbs. As a general rule, the leafy herbs (basil, mint, tarragon, parsley) are thrown in last, uncooked. The woody herbs (oregano, sage, rosemary, and thyme *"and then she'll be a true love of mine"* — Simon & Garfunkel) are cooked with the rest of the dish. You can tell if it's leafy or woody by looking at it. Also, the woody ones generally require you to strip the leaves off their "woody" stems.

Storage: Wrap leftover whole parsley, thyme, rosemary, mint, etc. in a paper towel and then plastic bag. This will give them a few extra days of life in the fridge. Pro tip: It works for leafy greens and lettuces too. For leftover unused "woody" (tee hee) herbs, wrap stems with a rubber band or string and hang upside down on a cabinet doorknob or a hook to dry. You'll then have a *bouquet garni* and air freshener all in one!

Also, our measurements on the herbs are generous. We've found that with many recipes, we wind up doubling, tripling, or further exponentially increasing the quantity of fresh herbs. I mean, what's the point of painstakingly washing, prepping, and chopping them if you're not even going to taste them in there, amirite?!?!

CILANTRO DISCLAIMER:

Cilantro is a vile, awful, poisonous weed garnered by the devil and has no place in this book, my kitchen, or the world. It will not appear anywhere in these recipes, not even the guacs, (especially the guacs!!!). If you happen to be part of the 75% of people that don't get this and are blissfully immune to its toxic offense, don't worry, you're not crazy; you just don't have the same old, wise genes that 25% of the population and I do. Also, you might be crazy, but that's a separate issue entirely. Please don't tell me if you insist on throwing it in—but do the right thing and check with your guests first.

A NEW YORK STATE OF MIND (AND MOUTH):

A favorite tried-and-true, consistently reliable source of side-splitting laughter and delight for me is saying things in my native New York accent. Case in point, the word "toss." While the adult California version of Jordan pronounces it like "tauss," back in deep New York, it comes out more like the number "two" followed by the pronoun "us," quickly combined. Try it, it's fun. "Two-us!"

Also fun from Jim: "Oo-wuhl goo-wuhn" (All gone)

From Betti: "This soo-wus is oo-wus-im" (This sauce is awesome)

You've got the hang of it now, riiiight?

TIME ESTIMATES:

I don't know how fast you chop. What do I know? Maybe you have knife skills like a character out of a Tarantino movie or maybe you drift off and solve a *WSJ* math problem in your head while knitting a scarf between slices. Time estimates are provided mainly to give you some idea if you can whip it up within an hour or so, if you need extra prep time (as for the tart dough), or if it's an overnight planning sitch (like the lox).

KITCHEN EQUIPMENT:

I learned how to cook when I was a very stable, well-adjusted, and single "starving artist." This doesn't mean I didn't have my shit together, but it does mean I only had one pot and one pan to work with. Therefore, I'm not going to specify the size of cookware in this book because: a) I never knew how big my pan was, and when I would read a recipe, I'd get stressed out by the limitation, fearing it was the wrong size, and then start downspiraling, wondering if I should house a measuring tape in a kitchen drawer; and b) you can make most recipes work with your one pot and pan from your twenties. The quality of your ingredients and seasoning will affect the outcome of your dishes far more than your pan size will. Most of the standard-sized pots, pans, sheets, and dishes will work. If you're halving the recipe go smaller, if you're doubling it go bigger. You guys got this part. Let's recap: Size matters, but there's an acceptable range you can work with.

"There was long ones, tall ones, short ones, brown ones; Black ones, round ones, big ones, crazy ones"
— War, "Spill the Wine"

CHEF'S LAGNIAPPE LESSONS:

May I please introduce you to the "*lagniappe*" (pronounced "lan-yap"): a little sumpin' sumpin' extra, a bonus, a gift. It's a Creole term that I picked up in New Orleans, and since that city had such a profound effect on my life, I felt it was only appropriate to pay homage to it. In the course of developing the recipes, I found opportunities to provide a little further explanation, a little chef's note, an extra tip. Where appropriate (or perhaps sometimes inappropriate, if I'm doing my job right), you will find a Chef's Lagniappe Lesson as a little bonus of information to help you with the recipes, for good measure. Geaux to town with them!

"Feel good music, I've been told Good for your body and it's good for your soul Gonna do it now Hey, hey, hey, hey Hey, Pocky-Way"
— The Meters, "Hey Pocky-Way"

OPP — OTHER PROMINENT PRODUCERS:

We've recommended a specific wine to pair with each dish. Sometimes you might not be able to find it. Sometimes you might have a different budget in mind. Sometimes you might just want to be contrary. For these and other reasons, we'd like to draw your attention to the OPP (Other Prominent Producers) section, where you'll find other similar selections when it comes to grape, region, and style. It's the list of Other Prominent Producers we're down with, and they're all naughty by nature.

"Who's down with OPP? (Every last homie)"
— Naughty by Nature, "O.P.P."

OK, you're ready now. Off you go. Does anyone else hear some "Pomp and Circumstance" in the background? I know. Me too.

TABLE OF CONTENTS

WINE TABLE OF CONTENTS

RED   WHITE   ROSÉ   ORANGE   SPARKLING   SPARKLING RED   DESSERT WINE

SUMMER

APPETIZERS

SALADS

MAINS

SIDES & SAUCES

DESSERTS & COCKTAILS

FALL

APPETIZERS

SALADS

MAINS

SIDES & SAUCES

DESSERTS & COCKTAILS

WINE LIST

REDS

NORTH AMERICA | USA

California

Turley, Zinfandel, *Paso Robles* .... WINTER - Soup, 37
Steele .... OPP, 37
Hammersky .... OPP, 37
Adelaida .... OPP, 37
Enfold, Anita's Blend, *Paso Robles* .... SPRING - Guac, 54
Daou .... OPP, 54
Law .... OPP, 54
Brecon .... OPP, 54
L'Aventure, Grenache/Syrah, *Paso Robles* .... SPRING - Pasta, 131
Denner .... OPP, 131
Clos Solene .... OPP, 131
Thacher .... OPP, 131
Broc Cellars .... OPP, 131
Linne Calodo, GSM, *Paso Robles* .... SUMMER - Tomato Sauce, 174
Hearst Ranch .... OPP, 174
Herman Story .... OPP, 174
Torrin .... OPP, 174
The Blending Lab, Syrah, *Paso Robles* .... FALL - Crumble, 187
Justin .... OPP, 187
Epoch .... OPP, 187
Booker .... OPP, 187
Stag's Leap, Cabernet Sauvignon, *Napa Valley* .... WINTER - Caesar, 76
Dunn .... OPP, 76
Mayacamas .... OPP, 76
Spottswoode .... OPP, 76
Shafer, Cabernet Sauvignon, *Napa Valley* .... FALL-Steak, 119
Cade .... OPP, 119
Plumpjack .... OPP, 119
Heitz .... OPP, 119
The Prisoner, Zin Blend, *Napa Valley* .... WINTER - Meatball, 121
Orin Swift .... OPP, 121
Gamble Family .... OPP, 121
Day .... OPP, 121
Jordan, Cabernet Sauvignon, *Sonoma Valley* ..... WINTER - Spinach, 89
Corison .... OPP, 89
Coppola .... OPP, 89
Banshee .... OPP, 89
Mathis, Grenache, *Sonoma Valley* .... FALL - Spinach, 93
Dashe .... OPP, 93
Bonny Doon .... OPP, 93
Birichino .... OPP, 93
Rochioli, Pinot Noir, *Sonoma Valley* .... WINTER - Fish, 98
Littorai .... OPP, 98
Kistler .... OPP, 98
Claypool Cellars .... OPP, 98
Capiaux .... OPP, 98
Scribe, Nouveau Pinot Noir, *Sonoma Valley* ..... FALL - Tomato Sauce, 177
Division .... OPP, 177
Lo-Fi .... OPP, 177
Cep .... OPP, 177

Brander, Red Blend, *Santa Ynez Valley* .... FALL - Dutch Baby, 51
Jonata .... OPP, 51
Habit .... OPP, 51
Evan's Ranch .... OPP, 51
Helmet Red, Grenache Blend, *Santa Barbara* ... FALL - Ginger-Garlic, 154
Sine Qua Non .... OPP, 154
Whitcraft .... OPP, 154
Pax Mahle .... OPP, 154
The Valley Project, Counoise, *Santa Barbara* ... SPRING - Crumble, 182
Sea Smoke .... OPP, 182
Epiphany .... OPP, 182
AM/FM .... OPP, 182
La Clarine Farm, Syrah, *Sierra Foothills* .... SPRING - Caesar, 77
Haarmeyer .... OPP, 77
Terre Rouge .... OPP, 77

Oregon

Siduri, Pinot Noir, *Willamette Valley* .... FALL - Soup, 43
Adelsheim .... OPP, 43
Lingua Franca .... OPP, 43
Beaux Frères .... OPP, 43
Cristom .... OPP, 43
Sokol Blosser, Pinot Noir, *Willamette Valley* .... SPRING - Dutch Baby, 47
Brick House .... OPP, 47
Domaine Drouhin .... OPP, 47
Ken Wright .... OPP, 47
Hayden Fig .... OPP, 47

Mexico

Finca La Carrodilla, Bordeaux Blend, *Valle de Guadalupe* .. FALL - Guac, 58
Monte Xanic .... OPP, 58
Adobe Guadalupe .... OPP, 58

SOUTH AMERICA

Chile

Lapostolle, Bordeaux Blend, *Colchagua Valley* .... FALL - Chicken, 111
TerraNoble .... OPP, 111
Montes .... OPP, 111
Casa Silva .... OPP, 111

Argentina

Catena, Malbec, *Mendoza* .... WINTER - Steak, 114
Poesia .... OPP, 114
Andeluna .... OPP, 114
Chakana 'Cueva de las Manos' .... OPP, 114
Bodega Cicchitti .... OPP, 114

EUROPE

France

Domaine Jean Foillard, Gamay, *Beaujolais* .... SUMMER - Fish, 100
Domaine Lapierre .... OPP, 100
Guy Breton .... OPP, 100
Mee Godard .... OPP, 100
Olivier Merlin .... OPP, 100
Julie Balagny .... OPP, 100

Domaine Tempier, Mourvèdre, Bandol...............FALL - Meatball, 126
Château de Pibarnon..OPP, 126
La Bastide Blanche..OPP, 126
Château Pradeaux...OPP, 126
Bastide de la Ciselette..OPP, 126
Vieux Télégraphe, Rhône Blend, Châteauneuf-du-Pape
....FALL - Lemon-Dill, 151
Château de Beaucastel...OPP, 151
Château Rayas..OPP, 151
Domaine du Pegau..OPP, 151
Les Pallières, Rhône Blend, Gigondas................WINTER - Quinoa, 137
Santa Duc..OPP, 137
Saint Cosme...OPP, 137
Domaine du Grand Montmirail..OPP, 137
Olga Raffault, Cabernet Franc, Loire Valley........SPRING - Steak, 115
Bernard Baudry...OPP, 115
Catherine et Pierre Breton...OPP, 115
Jacky Blot..OPP, 115
Domaine Laporte...OPP, 115
Julien Pineau, Pineau, Loire Valley........SPRING - Tomato Sauce, 173
Brendan Tracey...OPP, 173
Domaine de la Roche Bleue..OPP, 173
La Grapperie...OPP, 173
Axel Prüfer, Natural Red Blend, Languedoc......WINTER - Cookie, 189
Mas Coutelou..OPP, 189
Henri Milan..OPP, 189
Chantereves L'Intrus...OPP, 189
Nicolas Carmarans, Fer Servadou, Aveyron..........FALL - Caesar, 80
L'Enclos des Braves..OPP, 80
Domaine Plageoles...OPP, 80
Domaine du Cros...OPP, 80
Château Flotis, Negrette, Fronton............................FALL - Pasta, 135
Château Bellevue la Forêt..OPP, 135
Château Coutinel...OPP, 135
Château Bouissel...OPP, 135

Italy
Antinori, Sangiovese, Tuscany...................SUMMER - Dutch Baby, 48
Ruffino..OPP, 48
Castello di Ama..OPP, 48
Fontodi...OPP, 48
Le Ragnaie...OPP, 48
Poggio Antico, Sangiovese, Tuscany.................WINTER - Chicken, 105
Altesino...OPP, 105
Casanove di Neri...OPP, 105
La Torre..OPP, 105
Bruno Giacosa, Nebbiolo, Piedmont..................WINTER - Pasta, 128
Ceretto...OPP, 128
Renato Ratti...OPP, 128
Flavio Roddolo...OPP, 128
Frank Cornelissen, Natural Blend, Sicily............SUMMER - Pesto, 167
Girolamo Russo..OPP, 167
Tenuta delle Terre Nere...OPP, 167
Passopisciaro...OPP, 167
Di Govanna..OPP, 167

Spain
Bodegas Arzuaga, Tempranillo, Ribera del Duero......FALL - Tart, 71
Vega Sicilia..OPP, 71
Emilio Moro...OPP, 71
Viña Sastre..OPP, 71
Fronton De Oro, Blend, Gran Canaria......SPRING - Ginger-Garlic, 157
Los Bermejos..OPP, 157
Envinate..OPP, 157
Tajinaste...OPP, 157
Bodegas Juan Gil, Monastrell, Jumilla....WINTER - Tomato Sauce, 172
Bodegas El Nido..OPP, 172
Clos Mogador...OPP, 172
Torres...OPP, 172

DOWN UNDER
Australia
Two Hands, Shiraz, Barossa Valley.....................WINTER - Guac, 53
Yalumba..OPP, 53
Penfolds..OPP, 53
Langmeil...OPP, 53
Mollydooker, Shiraz, Barossa Valley...................WINTER - Tart, 67
Henschke...OPP, 67
Shaw + Smith...OPP, 67
d'Arenberg...OPP, 67
Torbreck, GSM, Barossa Valley.......................SUMMER - Steak, 118
Clarendon Hills...OPP, 118
Dandelion..OPP, 118
Shinas Estates...OPP, 118

New Zealand
Felton Road, Pinot Noir, Central Otago..........SUMMER - Chicken, 108
Quartz Reef..OPP, 108
Pegasus Bay...OPP, 108
Two Paddocks...OPP, 108

AFRICA
South Africa
Lammershoek, Pinotage, Swartland...............WINTER - Crumble, 181
Kanonkop..OPP, 181
Simonsig...OPP, 181
Lievland..OPP, 181

WINE LIST

WHITES

USA

<u>California</u>

Uproot, Grenache Blanc, *Edna Valley*...........SUMMER - Spinach, 92
Donkey & Goat..OPP, 92
Tablas Creek Vineyard..OPP, 92
Coquelicot, Blend, *Los Olivos*.................WINTER - Dutch Baby, 46
Foley..OPP, 46
Dierberg..OPP, 46
Sanford...OPP, 46
Halleck, Gewürztraminer, *Sonoma Valley*............FALL - Quinoa, 142
Stony Hill...OPP, 142
Navarro...OPP, 142
Castello di Amorosa...OPP, 142
Cordon, Sauvignon Blanc, *Santa Barbara*......SUMMER - Lemon-Dill, 150
Arrow & Branch...OPP, 150
Prisma...OPP, 150
Gainey...OPP, 150
St. Suprey..OPP, 150

<u>Oregon</u>

Domaine Serene, Chardonnay, *Willamette Valley*...SPRING - Spinach, 90
Gran Moraine...OPP, 90
Walter Scott..OPP, 90
Evening Land...OPP, 90

<u>New York</u>

Channing Daughters, Blend, *Long Island*.............SPRING - Fruit, 83
Lieb Family Cellars...OPP, 83
Wölffer Estate...OPP, 83
Macari...OPP, 83

EUROPE

<u>France</u>

Zind-Humbrecht, Gewürztraminer, *Alsace*..........SPRING - Soup, 39
Hugel...OPP, 39
Trimbach...OPP, 39
Emile Beyer...OPP, 39
Domaine Marcel Deiss...OPP, 39
La Grange aux Belles, Chenin Blanc, *Loire Valley*...SPRING - Tart, 68
François Chidaine..OPP, 68
Benoit Courault...OPP, 68
Nicolas Joly..OPP, 68
Chave's Hermitage, Rhône Blend, *Rhône Valley*....SPRING - Fish, 99
E. Guigal...OPP, 99
Famille Perrin...OPP, 99
M. Chapoutier..OPP, 99
Château-Grillet, Viognier, *Rhône Valley*.................WINTER - Lox, 60
Tardieu-Laurent..OPP, 60
Christophe Pichon...OPP, 60
Pascal Cotat, Sauvignon Blanc, *Sancerre*................FALL - Lox, 65
Pascal Jolivet..OPP, 65

Lucien Crochet..OPP, 65
Louis-Benjamin Dagueneau...OPP, 65
Pierre Luneau-Papin, Melon de Bourgogne, *Muscadet*...FALL - Fish, 103
Domaine de l'Ecu..OPP, 103
Domaine de la Pépière..OPP, 103
Domaine du Haut Bourg..OPP, 103

<u>Italy</u>

Terredora di Paolo, Falanghina, *Campania*..............FALL - Fruit, 86
Fattoria La Rivolta..OPP, 86
Feudi di San Gregorio...OPP, 86
Quintodecimo..OPP, 86
Vigne Surrau, Vermentino, *Sardinia*.................SPRING - Quinoa, 138
Argiolas..OPP, 138
Siddura..OPP, 138
Capichera..OPP, 138
J. Hofstätter, Pinot Bianco, *Alto Adige*.................SUMMER - Lox, 62
Cantina Terlano...OPP, 62
Alois Lageder..OPP, 62
Tiefenbrunner..OPP, 62
Ronco del Gelso, Riesling, *Friuli-Venezia*......SPRING - Lemon-Dill, 148
Mitja Sirk..OPP, 148
Element...OPP, 148
Knebel...OPP, 148

<u>Spain</u>

Mar de Frades, Albariño, *Rías Baixas*.............SUMMER - Caesar, 79
Palacio de Fefiñanes...OPP, 79
Pazo de Señorans..OPP, 79
Zarate..OPP, 79

<u>Portugal</u>

Caves de Cerca, Vinho Verde, *Minho*.............SUMMER - Pasta, 132
Soalheiro...OPP, 132
Casa do Valle..OPP, 132
Anselmo Mendes...OPP, 132
Cartuxa, Blend, *Alentejo*....................WINTER - Lemon-Dill, 147
Esporão...OPP, 147
Cortes de Cima..OPP, 147
Mouchão..OPP, 147

<u>Germany</u>

J.J. Prüm, Riesling, *Mosel*.....................FALL - Ginger-Garlic, 160
S.A. Prüm..OPP, 160
Egon Müller...OPP, 160
Dr. Loosen...OPP, 160

<u>Greece</u>

Gaia, Assyrtiko, *Santorini*...........................SUMMER - Quinoa, 140
Hatzidakis...OPP, 140
Boutari..OPP, 140
Domaine Sigalas...OPP, 140

AFRICA
South Africa
Mulderbosch, Sauvignon Blanc, *Stellenbosch*.....SUMMER - Tart, 69
Buitenverwachting...OPP, 69
Bayten...OPP, 69
Simonsig...OPP, 69

OCEANA
New Zealand
Cloudy Bay, Sauvignon Blanc, *Marlborough*........SUMMER - Guac, 56
Clos Henri..OPP, 56
Greywacke..OPP, 56
Seresin..OPP, 56

ROSÉ

California
Margerum Wine Company, Riviera, *Santa Barbara*...SUMMER - Soup, 40
A Tribute to Grace..OPP, 40
Stolpman...OPP, 40
Julien Fayard..OPP, 40
Kunin, Phoebe, *Santa Barbara*.....................SPRING - Meatball, 122
Red Car...OPP, 122
Matthiasson..OPP, 122
Peay..OPP, 122

Germany
Wagner-Stempel, Rosé, *Rheinhessen*................SUMMER - Fruit, 84
Künstler..OPP, 84
von Winning..OPP, 84
Leitz..OPP, 84

Oregon
Penner-Ash, Rosé, *Willamette Valley*.................SUMMER - Cookie, 192
Bow & Arrow...OPP, 192
Stoller...OPP, 192
TellTale...OPP, 192

France
Domaine de Terrebrune, Rosé, *Bandol*..............SPRING - Lox, 61
Domaine le Galantin...OPP, 61
Domaine La Suffrene...OPP, 61
Clos Cibonne..OPP, 61

ORANGE

Italy
Denavolo, Catavela, *Emilia-Romagna*.............SPRING - Chicken, 106
Movia..OPP, 106
Kabaj..OPP, 106
La Stoppa...OPP, 106

BUBBLES

France
Philippe Foreau, Vouvray, *Loire Valley*................WINTER - Fruit, 82
Domaine Huet...OPP, 82
Champalou...OPP, 82
François Pinon..OPP, 82

Italy
Podere il Saliceto, Bi Fri, *Emilia-Romagna*.....SUMMER - Meatball, 124
Ca' dei Zago...OPP, 124
La Staffa...OPP, 124
Bisson...OPP, 124
Opera 02, Lambrusco di Modena, *Emilia-Romagna*...WINTER - Pesto, 163
Cleto Chiarli...OPP, 163
Fiorini...OPP, 163
Medici Ermete..OPP, 163
Ca' del Bosco, Cuvee Prestige, *Lombardy*..........SPRING - Pesto, 164
Berlucchi..OPP, 164
Barone Pizzini...OPP, 164
Flor, Prosecco, *Veneto*........................SUMMER - Ginger-Garlic, 158
Zardetto..OPP, 158
Le Colture...OPP, 158
Bisol...OPP, 158

Spain
Bidaia Txakolina, Hondarrabi Zuri, *Getariako*...........FALL - Pesto, 168
Ameztoi...OPP, 168
Mokoroa..OPP, 168
Txomin Etxaniz..OPP, 168

California
Frank Family Vineyards, Rouge, *Carneros*.....SUMMER - Crumble, 184
The Chook..OPP, 184
Ryme..OPP, 184

DESSERT

Canada
Inniskillin, Ice Wine, *Niagara Peninsula*.................FALL - Cookie, 193
Mission Hill...OPP, 193
Peller Estates...OPP, 193
Wayne Gretsky Estates...OPP, 193

France
Chateau D'Yquem, Late Harvest, *Sauternes*......SPRING - Cookie, 190
Château Guiraud...OPP, 190
Château Doisy Daëne..OPP, 190
Château Suduiraut..OPP, 190

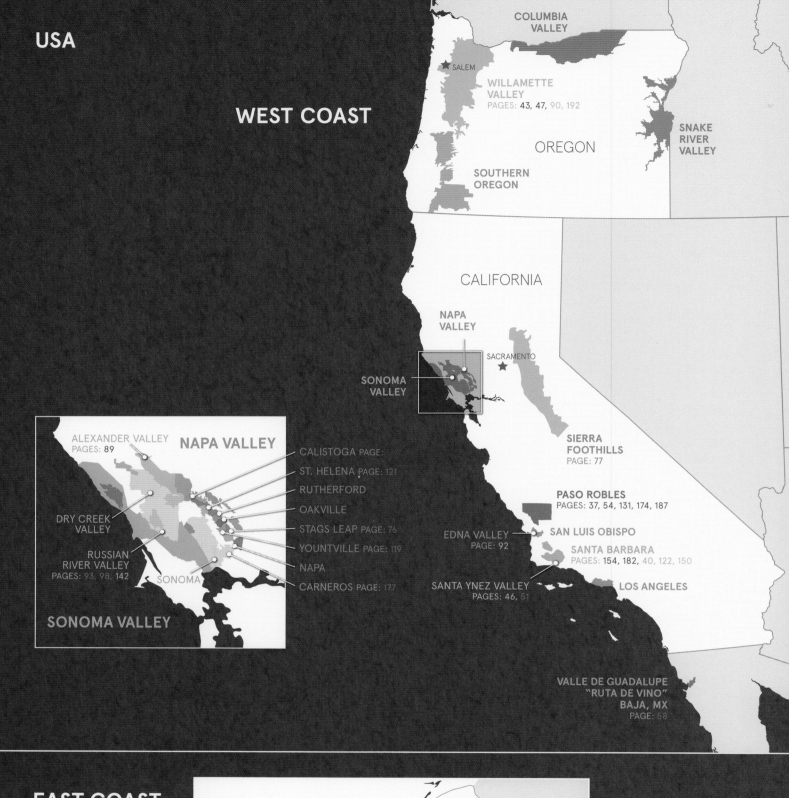

USA

WEST COAST

COLUMBIA
VALLEY

SALEM

WILLAMETTE
VALLEY
PAGES: 43, 47, 90, 192

OREGON

SNAKE
RIVER
VALLEY

SOUTHERN
OREGON

CALIFORNIA

NAPA
VALLEY

SACRAMENTO

SONOMA
VALLEY

SIERRA
FOOTHILLS
PAGE: 77

NAPA VALLEY

ALEXANDER VALLEY
PAGES: 89

CALISTOGA PAGE:

ST. HELENA PAGE: 121

RUTHERFORD

OAKVILLE

DRY CREEK
VALLEY

STAGS LEAP PAGE: 76

YOUNTVILLE PAGE: 119

RUSSIAN
RIVER VALLEY
PAGES: 93, 98, 142

NAPA

SONOMA

CARNEROS PAGE: 177

SONOMA VALLEY

PASO ROBLES
PAGES: 37, 54, 131, 174, 187

EDNA VALLEY
PAGE: 92

SAN LUIS OBISPO

SANTA BARBARA
PAGES: 154, 182, 40, 122, 150

SANTA YNEZ VALLEY
PAGES: 46, 51

LOS ANGELES

VALLE DE GUADALUPE
"RUTA DE VINO"
BAJA, MX
PAGE: 58

EAST COAST

ONTARIO

PRINCE
EDWARD
COUNTY

NEW YORK

NIAGARA
PENINSULA
PAGE: 193

ALBANY

NORTHFORK

LAKE
ERIE
REGION

**FINGER
LAKES**

LAKE ERIE
NORTH
SHORE

**HUDSON
VALLEY**

LONG ISLAND
PAGE: 83

THE
HAMPTONS

N

CHILE AND ARGENTINA

SALTA

ATACAMA REGION

CATAMARCA

COQUIMBO REGION

LA RIOJA

ACONCAGUA REGION

SAN JUAN

SANTIAGO

MENDOZA
PAGE: 114

BUENOS AIRES

CENTRAL VALLEY REGION
COLCHAGUA   PAGE: 111

ARGENTINA

SOUTH REGION

NEUQUÉN

AUSTRAL REGION

CHILE

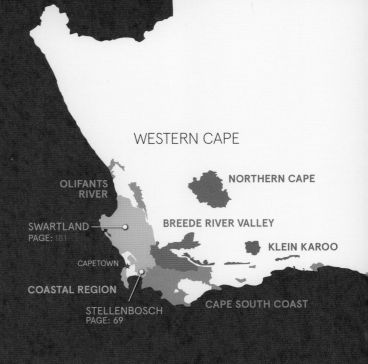

WESTERN CAPE

OLIFANTS
RIVER

NORTHERN CAPE

SWARTLAND
PAGE: 181

BREEDE RIVER VALLEY

KLEIN KAROO

CAPETOWN

COASTAL REGION

STELLENBOSCH
PAGE: 69

CAPE SOUTH COAST

SOUTH AFRICA

NEW ZEALAND

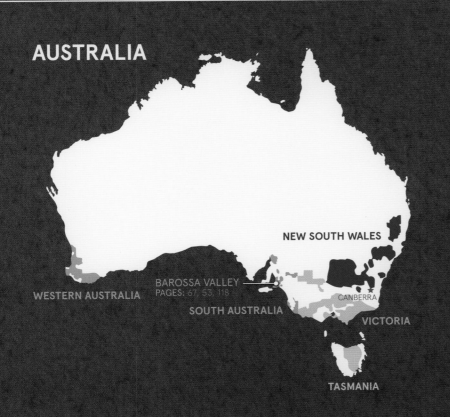

AUSTRALIA

NEW SOUTH WALES

BAROSSA VALLEY
PAGES: 67, 53, 118

CANBERRA

WESTERN AUSTRALIA

SOUTH AUSTRALIA

VICTORIA

TASMANIA

NELSON

WELLINGTON

SOUTH ISLAND

MARLBOROUGH
PAGE: 56

WAIPARA VALLEY / CANTERBURY

CENTRAL OTAGO
PAGE: 108

BANNOCKBURN

N

SPAIN AND PORTUGAL

GETARIAKO
TXAKOLINA
PAGE: 168

GALICIA

RIBERA DEL DUERO
PAGE: 71

BASQUE
COUNTRY

RÍAS BAIXAS
PAGE: 79

RIOJA

MINHO
PAGE: 132

ARAGON

VINHO
VERDE

CASTILLA Y LÉON

CATALONIA

★ MADRID

SPAIN

VALENCIA

LISBON ★

ALENTEJO
PAGE: 147

JUMILLA
PAGE: 172

MURCIA

CANARY ISLANDS

PORTUGAL

GRAN CANARIA
PAGE: 157

ANDALUCIA

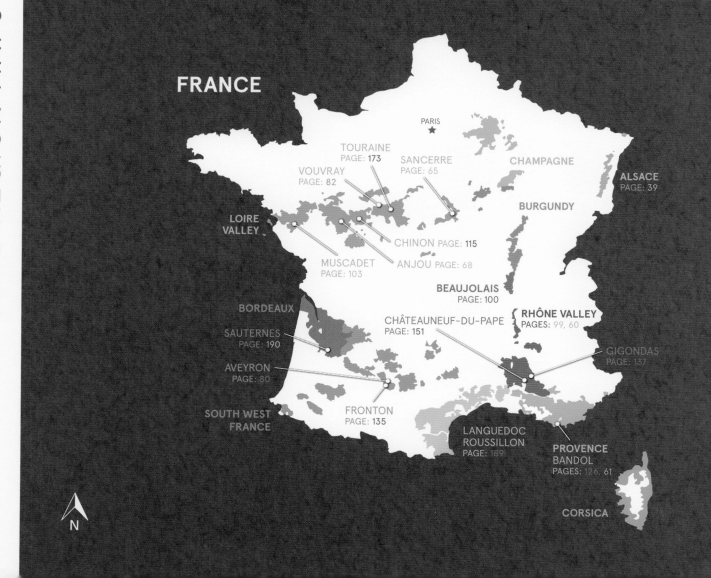

FRANCE

★ PARIS

TOURAINE
PAGE: 173

SANCERRE
PAGE: 65

CHAMPAGNE

VOUVRAY
PAGE: 82

ALSACE
PAGE: 39

LOIRE
VALLEY

BURGUNDY

CHINON PAGE: 115

MUSCADET
PAGE: 103

ANJOU PAGE: 68

BEAUJOLAIS
PAGE: 100

BORDEAUX

RHÔNE VALLEY
PAGES: 99, 60

SAUTERNES
PAGE: 190

CHÂTEAUNEUF-DU-PAPE
PAGE: 151

GIGONDAS
PAGE: 137

AVEYRON
PAGE: 80

SOUTH WEST
FRANCE

FRONTON
PAGE: 135

LANGUEDOC
ROUSSILLON
PAGE: 189

PROVENCE
BANDOL
PAGES: 126, 61

N

CORSICA

ITALY

LOMBARDY
PAGE: 164

ALTO ADIGE
PAGE: 62

FRIULI-VENEZIA GIULIA
PAGE: 148

PIEDMONT
PAGE: 128

VENETO
PAGE: 158

EMILIA ROMAGNA
PAGES: 106, 124,

TUSCANY
PAGES: 48, 105

ROME

CAMPANIA
PAGE: 86

SARDINIA
PAGE: 138

SICILY
PAGE: 167

TUSCANY

MASSA-
CARRARA

LUCCA

LIVORNO

CHIANTI CLASSICO
PAGE: 48

CHIANTI

MONTALCINO
PAGE: 105

GROSSETO

GERMANY

BERLIN

MOSEL VALLEY
PAGE: 160

RHEINGAU

RHEINHESSEN
PAGE: 84

FRANKEN

NAHE

HESSISCHE
BERGSTRASSE

PFALZ

WURTTEMBERG

BADEN

GREECE

NORTHERN
GREECE

CENTRAL
GREECE

ATHENS

AEGEAN
ISLANDS

SOUTHERN
GREECE

SANTORINI
PAGE: 140

N

MUSIC TABLE OF CONTENTS

SUMMER

FALL

MUSIC LIST

Alanis Morissette, *Jagged Little Pill* (1995), Alt Rock...SPRING - Spinach, 90

Albert King, *Funky London* (1994), Funk Blues...SPRING - Pasta, 131

The Allman Brothers Band, *Eat a Peach* (1972), Southern Rock...SUMMER - Spinach, 92

Anders Osborne, *American Patchwork* (2010), Blues Rock...SUMMER - Ginger-Garlic, 158

Armik, *Rosas del Amor* (1987), Flamenco...SUMMER - Caesar, 79

The Band, *The Last Waltz* (1978), Rock...FALL - Ginger-Garlic, 160

The Beach Boys, *Pet Sounds* (1966), Pop Rock...SUMMER - Soup, 40

Beastie Boys, *Paul's Boutique* (1989), Hip-Hop...SUMMER - Steak, 118

The Beatles, *Abbey Road* (1969), Rock...SPRING - Dutch Baby, 47

Belle & Sebastian, *Tigermilk* (1996), Indie Pop...SPRING - Pesto, 164

Ben Harper, *Fight for Your Mind* (1995), Blues Rock...SUMMER - Lox, 62

The Big Chill Soundtrack (1983), Motown...SUMMER - Cocktail, 197

Bill Withers, *Lean on Me: The Best of Bill Withers* (1994), Soul...FALL - Spinach, 93

Billy Joel, *The Stranger* (1977), Rock...SPRING - Quinoa, 138

The Black Keys, *Rubber Factory* (2004), Rock...WINTER - Steak, 114

Bloomfield, Kooper, Stills, *Super Session* (1968), Blues Rock...SPRING - Soup, 39

Bob Dylan, *Blonde on Blonde* (1966), Folk Rock...WINTER - Dutch Baby, 46

Bob Marley, *Kaya* (1978), Reggae...SUMMER - Meatball, 124

Bruce Springsteen, *Born in the U.S.A.* (1984), Rock...SUMMER - Fish, 100

Cake, *Prolonging the Magic* (1998), Alt Rock...SPRING - Cookie, 190

Cannonball Adderley, *Somethin' Else* (1958), Jazz...FALL - Meatball, 126

Carole King, *Tapestry* (1971), Soft Rock...FALL - Dutch Baby, 51

Chris and Rich Robinson, *Brothers of a Feather: Live at the Roxy* (2007), Rock...FALL - Quinoa, 142

The Coup, *Sorry to Bother You Soundtrack* (2018), Hip-Hop...SUMMER - Guac, 56

Creedence Clearwater Revival, *Willy and the Poor Boys* (1969), Southern Rock...FALL - Tomato Sauce, 177

Crosby, Stills, Nash, & Young, *So Far* (1974), Classic Rock...SUMMER - Lemon-Dill, 150

Dave Matthews Band, *Under the Table and Dreaming* (1994), Rock...SUMMER - Quinoa, 140

David Bowie, *The Rise and Fall of Ziggy Stardust* (1972), Glam Rock...SPRING - Caesar, 77

Derek and the Dominos, *Layla and Other Assorted Love Songs* (1970), Blues Rock...WINTER - Ginger-Garlic, 154

The Derek Trucks Band, *Songlines* (2006), Blues Rock...SPRING - Meatball, 122

Dr. Dog, *Be The Void* (2012), Indie Rock...FALL - Caesar, 80

Dr. Dre, *2001* (2001), Hip-Hop...WINTER - Pesto, 163

Duran Duran, *Rio* (1982), Pop...SPRING - Crumb, 182

Edie Brickell & New Bohemians, *Shooting Rubberbands at the Stars* (1988), Folk Rock...FALL - Lox, 65

Ella Fitzgerald and Louis Armstrong, *Ella & Louis Christmas* (2016), Jazz...WINTER - Cookie, 189

Fitz and The Tantrums, *Pickin' Up the Pieces* (2010), Pop...FALL - Pesto, 168

Fleetwood Mac, *Rumours* (1977), Pop Rock...FALL - Guac, 58

Galactic, *Late for the Future* (2000), Funk...FALL - Cookie, 193

Glee! Soundtrack Vol. 1 (2009), Show Tunes...FALL - Crumble, 187

Grateful Dead, *American Beauty* (1970), Folk Rock...FALL - Soup, 43

APPETIZERS

SOUP

Soups are soul-warming. They are the perfect canvas for a base recipe and variable components. I'm not a huge hot food person—I'm really not as tough as I look. My mouth is super sensitive to temperatures; I have a lower threshold than most people. I walk around with a mini thermometer in my purse. True story. Most people can handle 160 degrees, but my mouth is singed and burned for a week if I dive into anything over 130. So, predictably, I enjoy the soups here both hot off the stove and then cooled to an ideal 125 degrees, or cold after they've enjoyed a visit to the fridge to chill. These are the Zucker faves for the seasons, but feel free to doctor them up to your tastes (add a roux to thicken, cream for body, or spices, soy sauce, different veggies, etc.).

Broccoli-Spinach Soup

PREP TIME: 15 MINUTES / TOTAL TIME: 45 MINUTES / SERVINGS: 6-8

¼ c olive oil

1 leek, white and light green parts only, thinly sliced

1 small yellow onion, chopped

2 garlic cloves, chopped (about 1 T)

1 head broccoli, chopped into bite-size pieces

Salt and pepper

2 bay leaves

2½ c chicken stock or broth

3 c fresh spinach (baby is OK)

Heat the olive oil in a massive pot over medium-high heat. Add the leek and onion and sauté for 2 minutes, with the occasional stir. The alliums (onion family) should start to soften and wilt. Add the garlic and continue sautéing until translucent (about another 2 minutes). Add the broccoli, 1½ teaspoons salt, 1 teaspoon pepper, and the bay leaves. Stir and cook until the broccoli is nice and bright green, about 2 minutes. (Instastory photo op optional.) Add the chicken stock and bring to a rolling boil. Lower the heat to simmer, cover, and let cook for 8 minutes, until tender. Remove and discard the bay leaves.

In batches, transfer the soup to a blender. Add some of the spinach to each batch and blend well, about 30 seconds per batch. Transfer each blended batch to a bowl and stir together. Season to taste. Slurp time.

CHEF'S LAGNIAPPE LESSON: With chopping leeks, much like my life in general, I just don't know when to stop. Thankfully, leeks are filthy beasts, dirty birds, gritty greens. When you slice them up, you'll usually start to hit a super-dirty spot at the darker green part, and this serves as a great visual cue for when you're supposed to stop slicing. I recommend soaking the slices in a bowl of cold water for a few minutes to wash them off—the dirt will sink to the bottom of the bowl—then drain and rinse.

CHEF'S LAGNIAPPE LESSON: Broths are a wonderful opportunity to add flavor to your dishes. Consider it the pillar of your dish. If the broth is bland, there is little the rest of the ingredients can do to save it. You don't have to be a big shot and make your own broth (though I don't discourage this), but make sure you use something worthy of its quiet hero status. Also, be wary of the chemicals and food coloring in some brands. My mother and I encourage going as natural as possible.

WINE: *Zinfandel*
PRODUCER: **Turley**
REGION: **Paso Robles, CA**
A jammy California Zinfandel is the perfect winter red, bold enough to wrap around you in the cold, but bright enough to work with a nice, soothing soup. Turley produces some of my favorite Zins from legit old vines dating back to the 19th and 20th centuries. Just like a well-matured human, old vines have built up their character and stability. An ex-boyfriend turned me on to the winery and, coincidentally, the arc of our relationship mimics the wine: super promising, good foundation, and a big finish that you'll be talking about for years.

OPP: **Steele, Hammersky, Adelaida**

BAND: **The Rolling Stones**
ALBUM: *Let It Bleed*
YEAR/GENRE: **(1969), Rock/Blues**
The Stones offer a wealth of choices from the depths of their rich album catalogue, but ultimately I chose *Let It Bleed*. Maybe it's because I fantasize about being a "Honky Tonk Woman." Or perhaps it's because "You Can't Always Get What You Want" reigns as a life mantra, especially on a cold winter day. Regardless, it'll reliably put the "rock" in your brockoli and "we all need someone [your soup] can lean on." P.S. I would imagine I'll keep my name when I get married, except if it would change to Jordan Jagger, because that's just inching toward perfection in every way.

Mint-Pea Soup

Mint-Pea Soup

PREP TIME: 15 MINUTES / TOTAL TIME: 45 MINUTES / SERVINGS: 6-8

. . . .

¼ c olive oil

1 leek, white and light green parts only, thinly sliced (see  page 37)

1 small yellow onion, chopped

2 garlic cloves, chopped (about 1 T)

1 (16-oz.) bag frozen peas (no need to defrost)

Salt and pepper

2 bay leaves

2½ c chicken stock or broth

2 T baby arugula

¾ c chopped fresh mint

. . . .

Heat the olive oil in a massive pot over medium-high heat. Add the leek and onion and sauté for 2 minutes, with the occasional stir. The alliums (onion family) should start to soften and wilt. Add the garlic and continue sautéing until translucent, about another 2 minutes. Add the peas and stir well until they turn bright green. Add 1½ teaspoons salt, 1 teaspoon pepper, and the bay leaves. Add the chicken stock and bring to a rolling boil. Lower the heat to simmer, cover, and let cook for 3 minutes, until tender. Remove and discard the bay leaves.

In batches, transfer the soup to a blender. Add some of the arugula and mint to each batch and blend well, about 30 seconds per batch. Transfer each blended batch to a bowl and stir together. Season to taste. Slurp time.

CHEF'S LAGNIAPPE LESSON: If anyone lurking around the kitchen, like maybe your dad, finds the arugula here too peppery, you can leave it out or use a milder green such as watercress (or simply ignore his complaints and carry on).

WINE: **Gewürztraminer**
PRODUCER: **Zind-Humbrecht**
REGION: **Alsace, France**
This dish, which seems deceptively simple, presents a flavor challenge. The distinctive pea and subtle mint flavors are actually difficult to match with wine. That's why I turn to the great white wine equalizer: Gewürztraminer. Not only is this wine fun to drink, but it's equally fun to say! "Guh-vertz-tra-mee-ner," colloquially known as Gewürz—not to be confused with one of my childhood friends from camp, Susan Gewirtz. It's a hearty, aromatic white grape originating from France's Alsace region, which lies in the northeastern part of the country, close to the German border. Structured but well-balanced, Gewürztraminer can stand up to strong flavors without overwhelming them.

OPP: **Trimbach, Emile Beyer, Hugel, Domaine Marcel Deiss**

BAND: **Mike Bloomfield, Al Kooper, Stephen Stills**
ALBUM: *Super Session*
YEAR/GENRE: **(1968), Blues Rock**
The rock in this one is thick like pea soup and the grooves are fresh like mint. It's perfect for your SOUPer Session! Guaranteed, one of my friends will add this album to their queue if they hear it at my house. Musical taste is one of those touchstones that you note when vetting a new acquaintance. I discovered this album independently from my dad, but when I played it in New York, he exclaimed, "How'd you hear of *Super Session*?! It's a great album!" (He often marvels at how I know music that was created before I was born, as if the music dies or hides a year after its release. Dads are so funny.) Fun fact: There's actually a second super session dubbed *Kooper Session* which features a 15-year old Shuggie Otis.

WINE: *Rosé*
PRODUCER: **Margerum**
REGION: **Santa Barbara, CA**
I'm not one to rosé all day in the summer. Wait, that might be a lie. It certainly happens. But I'm just as likely to drink white all night or red 'til bed. Moving on from my failed attempt at a disclaimer, this summer soup is screaming for a nice chilled rosé. This one is primarily a blend of Grenache and Syrah, which is typical for the warm Santa Barbara region. This wine sees some barrel fermentation for added flavor and girth, which sets it apart from the typical, light Provençal rosé French counterpart (all tank, no barrel). Girth matters. I discovered this one at W.I.N.O. in New Orleans, my ritual stop to stock the room upon MSY (Louis Armstrong New Orleans International Airport) arrival. The four bottles purchased for the long weekend proved to be insufficient. Just sayin'.

OPP: **A Tribute to Grace, Stolpman Vineyards, Julien Fayard 'Azur'**

BAND: **The Beach Boys**
ALBUM: *Pet Sounds*
YEAR/GENRE: **(1966), Pop Rock/Psychedelic Rock**
"Sloop John B" is one of the top 10 Zucker sing-alongs. We'll sprinkle and hide a few throughout the book. See if you can find all of them on the unofficial Zucker sing-along treasure hunt. But back to the Beach Boys. What's a summer without some Beach Boys? They're essentially a musical incarnation of the June solstice (with a pinch of a *Stranger Things*-esque fractured reality) with those sweet harmonies and perfectly wrought melodies. Try not to get kicked out of the San Diego Zoo when you're slurping your soup like an animal—unlike the Beach Boys album cover shoot legend.

Zucchini-Basil Soup

PREP TIME: 15 MINUTES   /   TOTAL TIME: 45 MINUTES   /   SERVINGS: 6-8

¼ c olive oil

1 leek, white and light green parts only, thinly sliced (see 🎭 page 37)

1 small yellow onion, chopped

2 garlic cloves, chopped (about 1 T)

3 medium zucchini, chopped into ½-inch pieces

Salt and pepper

2 bay leaves

2½ c chicken stock or broth

½ c fresh basil

Heat the olive oil in a massive pot over medium-high heat. Add the leek and onion and sauté for 2 minutes, with the occasional stir. The alliums (onion family) should start to soften and wilt. Add the garlic and continue sautéing until translucent, about another 2 minutes. Add the zucchini and stir well until starting to become translucent, about 2 minutes. Add 1½ teaspoons salt, 1 teaspoon pepper, and the bay leaves. Add the chicken stock and bring to a rolling boil. Lower the heat to simmer, cover, and let cook for about 8 minutes, until tender. Remove and discard the bay leaves.

In batches, transfer the soup to a blender. Add some of the basil to each batch and blend well, about 30 seconds per batch. Transfer each blended batch to a bowl and stir together. Season to taste. Slurp time.

CHEF'S LAGNIAPPE LESSON: If you'd like to thicken the soup up, you can include a potato (peeled and chopped) in the zucchini step, but I don't see the need to weigh down this light, summery dish with carbs unless you're super hungover. No judgment.

WINTER   SPRING   SUMMER   FALL

Butternut Squash–
Fennel Soup

Butternut Squash-Fennel Soup

PREP TIME: 1 HOUR 15 MINUTES / TOTAL TIME: 1 HOUR 45 MINUTES / SERVINGS: 6-8

1 medium butternut squash

SWOOPS

¼ c olive oil

1 leek, white and light green parts only, thinly sliced (see 🎭 page 37)

1 small yellow onion, chopped

2 garlic cloves, chopped (about 1 T)

1 fennel bulb, chopped, fronds removed

1 medium carrot, peeled and chopped

Salt and pepper

2 bay leaves

2½ c chicken stock or broth

Preheat the oven to 425°F. Slice the squash in half lengthwise and SWOOPS each half. Place on a foil-lined baking sheet and roast until the flesh can be easily scooped out of the shell, about 45 minutes. Remove from the oven and let cool.

Heat the olive oil in a massive pot over medium-high heat. Add the leek and onion and sauté for 2 minutes, with the occasional stir. The alliums (onion family) should start to soften and wilt. Add the garlic and continue sautéing until translucent, about another 2 minutes. Add the fennel, carrot, 1½ teaspoons salt, 1 teaspoon pepper, and the bay leaves. Stir well until the fennel starts to become translucent, about 2 minutes. Add the chicken stock and bring to a rolling boil. Lower the heat to simmer, cover, and let cook for about 8 minutes, until tender. Remove and discard the bay leaves.

In batches, transfer the soup to a blender. For each batch, scoop out some of the squash from the shell and add to the blender. Blend well, about 30 seconds per batch. Transfer each blended batch to a bowl and stir together. Season to taste. Slurp time.

CHEF'S LAGNIAPPE LESSON: I sometimes get fancy and serve the soup in an acorn squash bowl, which you can make by slicing across its equator and roasting in the oven while the butternut is getting it on in there too. Look at you, multitasking!

DUTCH BABY

When I was growing up, the kitchen was always my mother's domain, save for a few choice dishes on which my dad prided himself. One of his favorites was the Dutch baby breakfast pancake, which he often treated us to on lazy mornings when we were up relaxing at our mountain home in Vermont. We understand that everybody's favorite DNA test, 23andme, apparently detected a sweet tooth gene in my mom and me, but despite these genetic trait findings, we tend to prefer the salty road. So, naturally, my mom and I decided to transform this dish into some savory options, making them comparable to a quiche or a frittata. They're endlessly customizable, so go to town and make up your own flavor if you're so inspired!

Caramelized Onion & Blue Cheese Dutch Baby

PREP TIME: 30 MINUTES / TOTAL TIME: 1 HOUR 15 MINUTES / SERVINGS: 6-8

....

4 T unsalted butter

2 T olive oil

1 lb. yellow onions (about 4 small), finely chopped

2 T finely chopped parsley

Salt and pepper

½ c crumbled blue cheese

4 large eggs

1 c whole milk

1 c all-purpose flour

1 t freshly grated nutmeg

....

Preheat the oven to 475°F.

Melt the butter and olive oil in a 12-inch cast-iron skillet (or other oven-safe pan close to that size) over low heat. Add the onions and cook them until caramelized, about an hour, stirring occasionally. Season with the parsley, salt, and pepper. Turn off the heat. Sprinkle the blue cheese on top and make sure all of the ingredients are evenly distributed in the skillet.

In a blender, combine the eggs, milk, flour, nutmeg, 1 teaspoon salt, and ½ teaspoon pepper. Blend until smooth, about 30 seconds.

Slide the middle rack out of the oven and place the skillet in the center. Pour the batter into the skillet. Slowly slide the rack back into the oven (5 points for no spilling!) and cook until the Dutch baby is puffy and golden on top, 15 to 20 minutes. Remove the skillet from the oven immediately, slice the Dutch baby into wedges, and serve. The pancake will deflate after a few minutes, but it will still be just as delicious.

WINTER SPRING SUMMER FALL

Spinach, Leek & Gruyère Dutch Baby

PREP TIME: 30 MINUTES / TOTAL TIME: 1 HOUR 15 MINUTES / SERVINGS: 6-8

....

1 lb. fresh spinach

4 large eggs

1 c whole milk

1 c all-purpose flour

1 t freshly grated nutmeg

Salt and pepper

4 T unsalted butter

2 T olive oil

1 leek, white and light green parts only, thinly sliced (see  page 37)

¼ c grated Gruyère cheese, packed

....

Preheat the oven to 475°F.

Bring a large pot of lightly salted water to a boil. Add the spinach and blanch until wilted, about a minute. Drain the spinach and let cool. Squeeze dry (I like using a strainer or colander), coarsely chop, and set aside.

In a blender, combine the eggs, milk, flour, nutmeg, 1 teaspoon salt, and ½ teaspoon pepper. Blend until smooth, about 30 seconds.

Melt the butter and olive oil in a 12-inch cast-iron skillet (or other oven-safe pan close to that size) on medium-high heat. Add the leek and cook until tender and translucent, about 2 minutes. Add the chopped spinach and cook for an additional minute to warm through. Season with salt and pepper. Turn off the heat. Sprinkle the Gruyère on top and make sure all of the ingredients are evenly distributed in the skillet.

Slide the middle rack out of the oven and place the skillet in the center. Pour the batter into the skillet. Slowly slide the rack back into the oven (2 points for no spilling—it's not your first rodeo anymore) and cook until the Dutch baby is puffy and golden on top, 15 to 20 minutes. Remove the skillet from the oven immediately, slice the Dutch baby into wedges, and serve. The pancake will deflate after a few minutes, but it will still be just as delicious.

WINE: Pinot Noir
PRODUCER: **Sokol Blosser**
REGION: **Willamette Valley, OR**
When you all "Come Together" for lazy-day brunch, your "muddy water" for this dish should be a Pinot Noir, which is grown, produced, and "mojo filtered" in the Willamette Valley's Dundee Hills sub-region. Sokol Blosser practices sustainable, hands-on farming, making its wines super reliable from vintage to vintage, even through years with extreme climate fluctuations that would otherwise negatively impact the vulnerable, delicate, and finicky Pinot Noir grape. The juicy red cherry fruit will soften earthy Gruyère without clashing with the flavors of fresh spinach. Thanks to The Beatles' advanced arithmetic lesson, we all know "one and one and one is three." So have your one bite, one sip, and one song, come together, right now, over me. "The End."

OPP: **Brick House, Domaine Drouhin, Ken Wright, Hayden Fig**

BAND: **The Beatles**
ALBUM: *Abbey Road*
YEAR/GENRE: **(1969), Rock**
You really can't go wrong with any Beatles album, but this is Jim's fave along with *Sgt. Pepper's*. We may not be reinventing the wheel by appreciating breakfast with The Beatles (as evidenced by the ubiquitous namesake radio shows). Still, where the pairing lacks in originality, it dominates in virtue—starting the day with "Here Comes the Sun" is a reliable recipe for success. The Beatles is the No. 1 band that the entire Zucker family agrees on. (I will be dancing with my dad at my wedding one day to "I Feel Fine." Meaningful over traditional any day. It's how we roll.) Put The Fab Four on to round out your Tranquil Trio. You'll be singing "Oh! Darling" "I Want You" to your Dutch baby all morning long.

Roasted Tomato, Tarragon & Goat Cheese Dutch Baby

PREP TIME: 30 MINUTES / TOTAL TIME: 3 HOURS 15 MINUTES / SERVINGS: 6-8

1 pint yellow tear drop (pear) tomatoes (or yellow cherry tomatoes)

1 pint small red vine tomatoes (or red cherry tomatoes)

SWOOPS

4 large eggs

1 c whole milk

1 c all-purpose flour

1 t freshly grated nutmeg

Salt and pepper

4 T unsalted butter

1 t olive oil

¼ c crumbled goat cheese

½ c finely chopped fresh tarragon

Preheat the oven to 275°F.

Slice the tomatoes in half and place skin side down on a foil-lined baking sheet. SWOOPS and slow-roast in the oven until they're shriveled to half their original size, about 2 hours.

Crank that oven up to 475°F.

In a blender, combine the eggs, milk, flour, nutmeg, 1 teaspoon salt, and ½ teaspoon pepper. Blend until smooth, about 30 seconds.

Melt the butter and olive oil in a 12-inch cast-iron skillet (or other oven-safe pan close to that size) on medium-low heat. Turn off the heat. Arrange the tomatoes in the skillet in an evenly distributed layer. Evenly sprinkle the goat cheese and tarragon on top.

Slide the middle rack out of the oven and place the skillet in the center. Pour the batter into the skillet. Slowly slide the rack back into the oven (1 point for no spilling—you should be getting good by now...) and cook until the Dutch baby is puffy and golden on top, 15 to 20 minutes. Remove the skillet from the oven immediately, slice the Dutch baby into wedges, and serve. The pancake will deflate after a few minutes, but it will still be just as delicious.

CHEF'S LAGNIAPPE LESSON: Your standard produce carton is generally a pint (though raspberries are more commonly found in ½-pint cartons).

WINE: **Sangiovese**
PRODUCER: **Antinori**
REGION: **Chianti Classico, Italy**
This dish reminds me of Italian summers. A Tuscan Sangiovese to start the day? Yes, please. I'll be the "Lovingest Woman in Town" two sips in. With tart fruit and some tomato-like flavors of its own, Sangiovese is a classic pairing for anything acidic. The Sangiovese grape has rightfully become the darling Chianti Classico in the heart of Tuscany's hilly Chianti region. The Antinori family has been producing wine here for over 600 years—the vineyards are still family owned— they certainly have got this down!

OPP: **Ruffino, Castello di Ama, Fontodi, Le Ragnaie**

BAND: **Mumford & Sons**
ALBUM: *Babel*
YEAR/GENRE: **(2012), Folk Rock**
This little quartet of British lads formed in 2007 and create great music for lazy summer nights. Their debut *Sigh No More* was an instant classic like this wine thanks to songs like "The Cave" and "Little Lion Man" that capitalized on the burgeoning folk revival being led by bands like The Avett Brothers. I'm pretty sure the first time I saw these guys live was at High Sierra, which is the folkiest of the jam festivals you'll find. They're a great distraction while you're waiting for those tomatoes to roast on a lazy summer morning. Don't miss the bonus tracks on the deluxe version.

Roasted Tomato, Tarragon
& Goat Cheese Dutch Baby

Mushroom & Brie
Dutch Baby

Mushroom & Brie Dutch Baby

PREP TIME: 30 MINUTES / TOTAL TIME: 1 HOUR 15 MINUTES / SERVINGS: 6-8

. . . .

4 T unsalted butter

1 t olive oil

4 c sliced shiitake mushrooms (about 1 lb.)

Salt and pepper

Half of a 1-lb. wheel Brie cheese, rind removed, cut into little pieces (¼ c)

2 T finely chopped fresh thyme

4 large eggs

1 c whole milk

1 c all-purpose flour

1 t freshly grated nutmeg

. . . .

Preheat the oven to 475°F.

Melt the butter and olive oil in a 12-inch cast-iron skillet (or other oven-safe pan close to that size) on medium-high heat. Add the mushrooms and cook until tender, about 8 minutes. Sprinkle with salt and pepper. Turn off the heat. Sprinkle the Brie and thyme on top and spread everything evenly throughout the pan.

In a blender, combine the eggs, milk, flour, nutmeg, 1 teaspoon salt, and ½ teaspoon pepper. Blend until smooth, about 30 seconds.

Slide the middle rack out of the oven and place the skillet in the center. Pour the batter into the skillet. Slowly slide the rack back into the oven (Spilling? Who spills?) and cook until the Dutch baby is puffy and golden on top, 15 to 20 minutes. Remove the skillet from the oven immediately, slice the Dutch baby into wedges, and serve. The pancake will deflate after a few minutes, but it will still be just as delicious.

WINE: **Red Blend**
PRODUCER: **Brander 'F/Red'**
REGION: **Santa Ynez Valley, CA**
On a trip up to the Santa Ynez Valley, popularized by the movie *Sideways*—P.S. My dad doesn't drink Merlot either—this red was dubbed our "breakfast red." So, we're pairing it with something you can have for breakfast. While the region is typically known for its Rhône varieties like Syrah, this one boasts predominantly Bordeaux varieties, like Cabernet Sauvignon and Cabernet Franc. Though it is easy-drinking and inexpensive, the winery pays serious attention to this juice, making it an excellent value. Go visit the Brander estate when you're in Los Olivos and tell them I sent you for breakfast. (Don't do that—name-dropping is unattractive, and also, they don't know me.)

OPP: **Jonata, Habit Wine Co., Evan's Ranch**

BAND: **Carole King**
ALBUM: *Tapestry*
YEAR/GENRE: **(1971), Soft Rock**
I learned the words to every song on this album at camp, specifically Camp Vega in Maine. (Let the Jewish geography commence!) Carole swept the Grammys the year this album was released (old school for "dropped"): Album of the Year, Record of the Year, Song of the Year, and Best Female Pop Vocal Performance. (She was the first woman to win Record of the Year.) Joni Mitchell, James Taylor, and legendary backup singer Merry Clayton (of Stones fame) join on vocals. You'll feel the earth move under your feet for sure at the first bite of this autumnal Dutch baby. You probably won't have any Dutch baby leftovers, but if you do, you'll still love them tomorrow. Eat some now before "It's Too Late."

GUACAMOLE

Guac is always a crowd-pleaser at a party, and freshly made guac is in a whole different league than premade. Avocados beg to be consumed within hours of being sliced open (shelf life is not the naked avo meat's strong suit). While most unimaginative guacs are packing raw onion and cilantro, I eliminate those sources of contention, bad breath, and nausea, and instead add flavor in other ways. You'll find authentic variations like mine all over Mexico. And as far as avocados are concerned, I generally subscribe to the "go Haas or go home" school of thought. (Unless you can't find them and then any will do.) My guacamole can be served as a dip with pita or tortilla chips. You can add it to a taco bar or use it to top tuna—but I'm happy just to eat it with a spoon. Guac was one of the first things I taught myself how to make. I was in charge of the apps for our annual Sequoia Labor Day camping trip, when the S.F. and L.A. friend crews would meet in the middle, swat flies, hike around, and sing around the campfire. Try to keep up with the lyrics.

Bacon & Tomatillo
Guacamole

Bacon & Tomatillo Guacamole

PREP TIME: 30 MINUTES / TOTAL TIME: 40 MINUTES
SERVINGS: 8 (BUT SOMETIMES 1-2, NO JUDGMENT)

12 slices bacon

2 medium tomatillos

SWOOPS

2 Roma tomatoes,
diced and lightly salted

1 garlic clove, minced
(about 1½ t)

½ jalapeño, minced
(about 1 T)

4 avocados

1 T fresh lime juice
(about 1 lime)

Fry the bacon slices in a large skillet over medium heat. Flip after 10 minutes and continue frying until crispy. Transfer to a paper towel–lined plate. Once cooled, crumble the bacon into bits and set aside.

Heat a grill to medium-high. Slice the tomatillos in half horizontally along their equator and SWOOPS the flat, fleshy side (not the skin side). Place them flat side down on the grill and cook for about 10 minutes, until you see some nice dark char marks. Remove from the grill and dice into pieces that are the same size as your tomatoes (I usually go with a ½-inch chop).

Throw the tomatoes in a large bowl. Add the garlic and jalapeño and lightly mix. Halve and pit the avocados, then scoop out and chop the avocado meat and add to the bowl. SWOOPS. Add the lime juice and mix. Add the crumbled bacon and chopped tomatillos. Mix to evenly incorporate all of the ingredients. Season to taste. Time for a dip.

WINE: **Shiraz**
PRODUCER: **Two Hands
'Gnarly Dudes'**
REGION: **Barossa Valley,
Australia**
Smoky bacon calls for a big, also smoky Shiraz, the Australian version of the Syrah grape. I've heard it said that Shiraz is like a fiddle and Syrah is like a violin. Because of higher temperatures and the longer growing season in regions like Barossa, Australian Shiraz wines have become separated both linguistically and stylistically from their French counterparts, with jammier, bolder fruit flavors. My dad fell deep into an Australian Shiraz affair in the '90s, and nobody in the family complained about it. Two Hands makes fab wines in the Barossa Valley, like this one from their introductory Picture Series. Though larger in production, this wine doesn't sacrifice in quality, and the screw cap allows for easy access if the corkscrew seems too daunting for breakfast.

OPP: **Yalumba, Penfolds, Langmeil**

BAND: **Pearl Jam**
ALBUM: *Ten*
YEAR/GENRE: **(1991), Hard Rock**
Guac (a.k.a. avo jam) is an easy way to slip into a celebration, and Pearl Jam jumps right into that transition. This debut album immediately slid the band into the mainstream grunge scene. I got to see the band live in Barcelona on a recent trip to Spain and didn't shut up about how excited I was to rock out to Perlas de Marmelada the whole time. I also got to see Eddie Vedder in 2017 solo-headline a friend's festival in Louisville called Bourbon and Beyond. Eddie walked around with a spiral notebook and clearly meticulously studies his craft every day. He's a substantive, meaty musician, just like this guac.

Hearts of Palm & Poblano Guacamole

PREP TIME: 30 MINUTES / TOTAL TIME: 40 MINUTES
SERVINGS: 1 (GET YOUR OWN, THIS IS ALL FOR ME—OK, COULD ALSO SERVE 8.)

....

SWOOPS

2 poblano peppers

**2 Roma tomatoes,
diced and lightly salted**

**1 garlic clove, minced
(about 1½ t)**

**½ jalapeño, minced
(about 1 T)**

4 avocados

**1 T fresh lime juice
(about 1 lime)**

1 c hearts of palm,
drained and chopped

....

Preheat the oven to 425°F. SWOOPS the poblanos and roast until the skins are shriveling, about 30 minutes, rotating the peppers every 8 minutes or so. Remove from the oven and let cool. Pull off the stems, then remove and discard the seeds. Chop the remaining flesh of the peppers and set aside.

Throw the tomatoes in a large bowl. Add the garlic and jalapeño and lightly mix. Halve and pit the avocados, then scoop out and chop the avocado meat and add to the bowl. SWOOPS. Add the lime juice and mix. Add the hearts of palm and chopped poblanos. Mix to evenly incorporate all of the ingredients. Season to taste. Get on in there.

WINE: **California Blend**
PRODUCER: **Enfold Wines
'Anita's Blend'**
REGION: **Paso Robles, CA**

Made from Syrah, Zinfandel, and Cabernet Sauvignon grapes, this red blend is big enough to take on the meaty avocado in this guac, but still pleasant and fruity enough for a budding springtime snack. This is a low production wine, which can be interpreted to mean that it is either a winemaker's personal passion or one that is offered as a "lagniappe" to wine club members—either way, it's special. Paso's higher-alcohol reds (>15.4%, like this one) enhance spiciness because alcohol acts as a carrier for the capsicum, or spice, from peppers. I like my heat turned up to 11. If you're looking to curb the heat, go for a white instead.

OPP: **Daou Vineyards,
Law, Brecon**

BAND: **Robert Palmer**
ALBUM: **Sneakin' Sally
Through the Alley**
YEAR/GENRE: **(1974),
Rock/Funk/Jam**

Not only is this a stellar album from start to finish, but the woman on the album cover looks like it could be my mother coming out of Studio 54 in 1974 (ignoring the fact that Betti didn't have her curls back then). For a debut, the groove in this album is hot like poblanos, thanks largely to the legendary Meters and Allen Toussaint backing "Hearts of Palmer" who cut this in New Orleans and the Bahamas. That creamy yet tangy mood you're hearing? That's props to Little Feat's Lowell George who's all over this. "Everyone will start to cheer" when you put on your sailin' shoes for this one.

"You make me feel like I don't need another
Come on baby let's pull back the covers
And do our best to help one another
Find out how much fun we can get into life"
— *Robert Palmer "How Much Fun"*

Crab & Dill Guacamole

PREP TIME: 10 MINUTES / TOTAL TIME: 30 MINUTES
SERVINGS: TECHNICALLY 8, BUT YOU STILL DIDN'T MAKE ENOUGH

....

2 Roma tomatoes, diced and lightly salted

1 garlic clove, minced (about 1½ t)

½ jalapeño, minced (about 1 T)

4 avocados

SWOOPS

1 T fresh lime juice (about 1 lime)

1 c fresh crabmeat

½ c chopped dill

....

Throw the tomatoes in a large bowl. Add the garlic and jalapeño and lightly mix. Halve and pit the avocados, then scoop out and chop the avocado meat and add to the bowl. SWOOPS. Add the lime juice and mix. Add the crabmeat and dill. Mix to evenly incorporate all of the ingredients. Season to taste. Dive in head first.

Crab & Dill
Guacamole

WINE: **Bordeaux Blend**
PRODUCER: **Finca La Carrodilla**
'Así se va a las estrellas'
REGION: **Valle de Guadalupe, Mexico**

The Finca La Carrodilla winery is just south of the border in Mexico's Baja Peninsula, on the Ruta del Vino, which literally means "wine route" in Spanish. We grabbed our passports and hopped down there for a girls' weekend, and this one, a Bordeaux-style blend of Merlot, Cabernet Sauvignon, and Cabernet Franc, was our favorite of the lot. The wines in this region have a little salinity to them, which goes really well with an autumnal guac. The tannins play against the creamy, mouth-coating nature of the eggplant, while the touch of smoke from the grilling process offers a pleasant background for the wine's lovely fruit-forward characteristics.

OPP: **Monte Xanic, Adobe Guadalupe**

BAND: **Fleetwood Mac**
ALBUM: *Rumours*
YEAR/GENRE: **(1977), Pop Rock**

The bluesy roots of the band from the rhythm section Mick Fleetwood (drums) and John McVie (bass) are paralleling the autumn vibe here, and the soft-rock influences of Christine McVie (keys), Lindsay Buckingham (guitar), and Stevie Nicks (vocals) mimic the avo/ eggplant ingredients. This is the No. 1 album played at the Zucker house. There was a period of time when I literally played it every day when I was getting in the shower. Opener "Second Hand News" would get me bouncing around my room, and I was usually all clean and dried by "Go Your Own Way." "Never Going Back Again," my favorite, is what I like to call the "Little Martha" of *Rumours* (see the Summer Spinach Salad pairing, page 92): Short. Sweet. Happy. Dependable gratification with every taste—just like guac.

Grilled Eggplant & Red Onion Guacamole

PREP TIME: 35 MINUTES / TOTAL TIME: 45 MINUTES
SERVINGS: 8 FOR THE RECORD, 2 OFF THE RECORD

. . . .

SWOOPS

1 eggplant, sliced into ½-inch disks

1 red onion, sliced into ½-inch disks

2 Roma tomatoes, diced and salted

1 garlic clove, minced (about 1½ t)

½ jalapeño, minced (about 1 T)

4 avocados

1 T fresh lime juice (about 1 lime)

. . . .

Heat a grill to medium-high. SWOOPS the eggplant and red onion slices. Grill for about 15 minutes, flip, and then grill on the other side for another 15 minutes, until nicely charred. (I would keep the onion on for another 15 minutes, but my mother would argue with me because she doesn't like them softer and sweeter—and because she likes to argue with me.) Remove the veggies from the grill, dice, and set aside.

Throw the tomatoes in a large bowl. Add the garlic and jalapeño and lightly mix. Halve and pit the avocados, then scoop out and chop the avocado meat and add to the bowl. SWOOPS. Add the lime juice and mix. Add the diced grilled eggplant and red onion to the bowl. Mix to evenly incorporate all of the ingredients. Season to taste. You know what to do.

WINTER SPRING SUMMER **FALL**

CURED SALMON (LOX)

I get it, I'm Jewish, I'm supposed to love lox. I just didn't realize how easy it was to make myself! Thanks to a best friend with Russian ancestry, I gave it a shot. As long as you have a quality fish as your base, you'll never go store-bought again. It's an instant breakfast party star. The booze adds flavor and speeds up the cure. You can slice and serve it on a platter for a bagel spread, or it goes really well on mini toasts with a white creamy cheese and some herbs on top.

Vodka, Caraway
& Dill Lox

Bourbon-Sage Lox

PREP TIME: 15 MINUTES / TOTAL TIME: 24-36 HOURS (YES, THAT LONG)
SERVINGS: 12-16

1 c kosher salt

½ c light brown sugar, packed

1 T whole black peppercorns

¼ c yuzu zest

¼ c chopped fresh sage

1 salmon fillet, skin-on (4 lbs.)

¼ c bourbon

Combine all of the dry-cure ingredients in a medium bowl (that's everything but the salmon and bourbon). Place a piece of foil down, big enough to wrap around the entire fillet. Top with a piece of parchment paper and then a piece of plastic wrap. Sprinkle a third of the dry cure in the middle to create a bed for the fish. Place the salmon skin side down on the bed. Pour the rest of the dry cure over the fish to fully submerge and cover it. It'll look like a lot, because it is and it's supposed to. Pour the bourbon evenly over the entire thing. (It all swims more in the rub than in the booze.) Wrap the salmon tightly in each layer and transfer to a baking dish (or something else that will catch juice). Place a weight on the wrapped fish and put the entire situation in the fridge. Get creative with the weight: You can use bagged rice, paperweights, your old 1970s encyclopedia yearning for its sense of purpose, etc. Refrigerate overnight and flip after 12 hours. After another 12 hours, give it a check. Remove the fish from the fridge, open it up, and poke it. It's supposed to be firm around the edges but should still bounce back so there's a thin crust around the fish and it isn't dry all the way through. When this consistency has been achieved (usually in 24 to 36 hours, depending on how thick the fillet is and how much weight you have on it), rinse it off, pat dry, and thinly slice at an angle. You're welcome.

CHEF'S LAGNIAPPE LESSON: There really is no substitution for the elusive yuzu. If you can't find it, you could use another type of citrus, but it won't be the same recipe. Before giving up hope, check out a Japanese or other specialty market, order online (Googling works wonders), or heed my friends' ubiquitous advice (that I have yet to master): Simply ignore the yuzu—no texting, no nothing. Apparently this is supposed to intrigue the fruit and make it want to show up at your house.

Gin-Lavender Lox

PREP TIME: 15 MINUTES / TOTAL TIME: 24-36 HOURS (1,440-2,160 MINUTES)
SERVINGS: 12-16

. . . .

1 c kosher salt

½ c sugar

¼ c lemon zest (from
about 2 huge lemons)

¼ c dried lavender

1 T whole black peppercorns

1 salmon fillet, skin-on (4 lbs.)

¼ c gin

. . . .

Combine all of the dry-cure ingredients in a medium bowl (that's everything but the salmon and gin). Place a piece of foil down, big enough to wrap around the entire fillet. Top with a piece of parchment paper and then a piece of plastic wrap. Sprinkle a third of the dry cure in the middle to create a bed for the fish. Place the salmon skin side down on the bed. Pour the rest of the dry cure over the fish to fully submerge and cover it. It'll look like a lot, because it is and it's supposed to. Pour the gin evenly over the entire thing. (It all swims more in the rub than in the booze.) Wrap the salmon tightly in each layer and transfer to a baking dish (or something else that will catch juice). Place a weight on the wrapped fish and put the entire situation in the fridge. Get creative with the weight: You can use canned goods, bricks, spare bowling trophies, your old 1980s roller skate who's been feeling super neglected, etc. Refrigerate overnight and flip after 12 hours. After another 12 hours, give it a check. Remove the fish from the fridge, open it up, and poke it. It's supposed to be firm around the edges but should still bounce back so there's a thin crust around the fish and it isn't dry all the way through. When this consistency has been achieved (usually in 24 to 36 hours, depending on how thick the fillet is and how much weight you have on it), rinse it off, pat dry, and thinly slice at an angle. Happy birthday!

WINE: **Pinot Bianco**
PRODUCER: **J. Hofstätter**
REGION: **Alto Adige, Italy**
This dish has punch, so it needs a wine that is equally flavorful without being overwhelming. Pinot Bianco, a.k.a. Pinot Blanc in Italian, is a white wine from northern Italy's Alto Adige region. With a stunning backdrop of the Dolomite Mountains, Alto Adige is famous for its refreshing, well-balanced whites. Pinot Bianco tends to have ripe fruit and refreshing acidity, like its sibling Pinot Grigio, but it is a touch rounder and fuller-bodied, allowing it to stand up to the richness of the salmon in this dish. Known as one of the standard-bearers in the region, J. Hofstätter is a fourth-generation, family-owned winery.

OPP: **Cantina Terlano, Alois Lageder, Tiefenbrunner**

BAND: **Ben Harper**
ALBUM: *Fight for Your Mind*
YEAR/GENRE: **(1995), Folk Rock/Alt Rock/Blues Rock**
This is the sophomore album that really put Ben Harper on the map with some now-timeless tunes like "Burn One Down." He means pot and not arson, so the song's a surefire way to happily start the meal. This may or may not surprise you, but I'm not a morning person. It takes about an extra hour or two for my personality and sense of humor to kick in after my body wakes up. This album, thanks to Ben playing a special lap guitar called a Weissenborn guitar, has always helped ease the delayed normal-person transition and keeps that summer mood mellow.

Tequila-Basil Lox

PREP TIME: 15 MINUTES / TOTAL TIME: 24-36 HOURS (THAT'S 1 TO 1½ DAYS)
SERVINGS: 12-16

....

1 c kosher salt	¼ c chopped fresh basil	¼ c tequila
½ c sugar	**1 T whole black peppercorns**	
¼ c lime zest (from about 3 limes)	**1 salmon fillet, skin-on (4 lbs.)**	

....

Combine all of the dry-cure ingredients in a medium bowl (that's everything but the salmon and tequila). Place a piece of foil down, big enough to wrap around the entire fillet. Top with a piece of parchment paper and then a piece of plastic wrap. Sprinkle a third of the dry cure in the middle to create a bed for the fish. Place the salmon skin side down on the bed. Pour the rest of the dry cure over the fish to fully submerge and cover it. It'll look like a lot, because it is and it's supposed to be. Pour the tequila evenly over the entire thing. (It all swims more in the rub than in the booze.) Wrap the salmon tightly in each layer and transfer to a baking dish (or something else that will catch juice). Place a weight on the wrapped fish and put the entire situation in the fridge. Get creative with the weight: You can use bagged flour, a cast-iron pot, your old 1990 CD collection struggling to maintain its relevance, etc. Refrigerate overnight and flip after 12 hours. After another 12 hours, give it a check. Remove the fish from the fridge, open it up, and poke it. It's supposed to be firm around the edges but should still bounce back so there's a thin crust around the fish and it isn't dry all the way through. When this consistency has been achieved (usually in 24 to 36 hours depending on how thick the fillet is and how much weight you have on it), rinse it off, pat dry, and thinly slice at an angle. Congratulations!

Tequila-Basil Lox

Vodka, Caraway
& Dill Lox

Vodka, Caraway & Dill Lox

PREP TIME: 15 MINUTES / TOTAL TIME: 24-36 HOURS (REQUIRES AT LEAST
ONE NIGHT OF DEEP REM SLEEP) / SERVINGS: 12-16

1 c kosher salt

¼ c chopped fresh dill

1 salmon fillet, skin-on (4 lbs.)

½ c sugar

2 T caraway seeds

¼ c vodka

¼ c orange zest
(from 1 to 2 oranges)

1 T whole black peppercorns

Combine all of the dry-cure ingredients in a medium bowl (that's everything but the salmon and vodka). Place a piece of foil down, big enough to wrap around the entire fillet. Top with a piece of parchment paper and then a piece of plastic wrap. Sprinkle a third of the dry cure in the middle to create a bed for the fish. Place the salmon skin side down on the bed. Pour the rest of the dry cure over the fish to fully submerge and cover it. It'll look like a lot, because it is and it's supposed to. Pour the vodka evenly over the entire thing. (It all swims more in the rub than in the booze.) Wrap the salmon tightly in each layer and transfer to a baking dish (or something else that will catch juice). Place a weight on the wrapped fish and put the entire situation in the fridge. Get creative with the weight: You can use stones, a toaster, Jenga blocks, your laptop from 2 years ago that's already obsolete, etc. Refrigerate overnight and flip after 12 hours. After another 12 hours, give it a check. Remove the fish from the fridge, open it up, and poke it. It's supposed to be firm around the edges but should still bounce back so there's a thin crust around the fish and it isn't dry all the way through. When this consistency has been achieved (usually in 24 to 36 hours, depending on how thick the fillet is and how much weight you have on it), rinse it off, pat dry, and thinly slice at an angle. Eureka!

WINE: **Sauvignon Blanc**
PRODUCER: **Pascal Cotat**
REGION: **Sancerre, France**
Sancerre is a region in the eastern part of France's Loire Valley known for its Sauvignon Blanc, which happens to be my favorite white grape. Flinty and bright, this wine delivers the right combo of slap and soothe for a proper autumnal wake-up, washing the palate clean after every sip. This one's from the "damned mountains," Les Monts Damnés, an iconic single vineyard chiseled with sharp limestone which mirrors the bracing crispness of this style of Sauvignon Blanc.

OPP: **Pascal Jolivet, Lucien Crochet, Louis-Benjamin Dagueneau**

BAND: **Edie Brickell & New Bohemians**
ALBUM: ***Shooting Rubberbands at the Stars***
YEAR/GENRE: **(1988), Folk Rock**
"What I Am" is psyched to wash down some lox with my Sancerre while breathing the "Air of December." This is by far the band's first album. Also, this is by far the band's best album. It's chock-full of recognizable songs that compel gentle swaying like a happy hippie and keep you warm and fuzzy on a crisp fall day. If you're in need of catching up, I'm not a morning person, so I'm rarely aware of too many things during brunch. But I know what I know and these three pairings all go, if you know what I mean.

TOMATO VEGGIE TART

Many people find it intimidating to make doughs from scratch, but I encourage you not to back down from the challenge. This recipe is easy, approachable, and one I hope you'll return to repeatedly. It's a great vessel for any kind of savory tart. The use of semi-frozen olive oil here, like the use of frozen butter in a dessert tart, helps structure and form the dough. We all have our beloved vegetarian, #meatlessmonday contingency of friends, so these tarts serve as a great dish to satisfy those souls. Here are our four favorite combos with tomatoes and seasonal veggies.

Potato, Cheddar & Fennel Tart

Potato, Cheddar & Fennel Tart

PREP TIME: 2 HOURS 30 MINUTES / TOTAL TIME: 4 HOURS / SERVINGS: 6-8

CRUST:

2 c all-purpose flour

1 t salt

½ c olive oil, chilled in the freezer for 1 hour (it should be thick but pourable and still loose enough to stir)

6 T ice water

FILLING:

2 T olive oil

3 yellow onions, sliced into ¼-inch disks

2 fennel bulbs, sliced into ¼-inch disks

1 T apple cider vinegar

½ t finely chopped fresh rosemary

Salt and pepper

4 medium russet potatoes (about 1 lb.), sliced into ¼-inch disks

1 garlic clove, minced (about 1½ t)

½ c grated Cheddar cheese

2 tomatoes, sliced into ¼-inch disks and lightly salted

TO MAKE THE CRUST: Combine the flour and salt in a large food processor. Add the semi-frozen olive oil and blend. Add the ice water 1 tablespoon at a time with the motor running until a dough has formed. You're looking for a solid dough that holds together but isn't too sticky. You may need to adjust the amount of water due to factors like weather, altitude, time of month, etc. (maybe not time of month, but it's easy to blame that for things, Amirite?). Remove the dough from the processor and form it into a big disk. Wrap it in plastic and refrigerate for at least an hour.

TO MAKE THE TART: Heat 1 tablespoon olive oil on medium heat in a large skillet. Add the onions and fennel and cook until caramelized, about 30 minutes. Add the ACV and rosemary, season with salt and pepper, and stir to mix well. Remove from the heat, transfer to a bowl, and set aside. Heat the remaining 1 tablespoon olive oil on medium-high heat in the same skillet. Add the potatoes and season with salt (more than you think you should—potatoes need a lot of salt). Cook for about 10 minutes. Flip, add the garlic, and cook for another 10 minutes. Remove from the heat and set aside. Preheat the oven to 375°F. Spray a 12-inch tart pan with a removable bottom with cooking spray. Remove the dough from the fridge and place in the pan. Using your fingers, push the dough around and up the edge of the pan until it covers the entire pan evenly. Sprinkle the Cheddar on the bottom of the tart crust, then add the onions and fennel. Layer the potatoes and garlic on top, slightly overlapping to form a full layer. Finally, arrange the tomatoes on top—you can overlap them slightly in a spiral or rows or scatter them loosely for whichever tart look you're going for. Bake the tart in the oven for 30 minutes. Remove, let cool, and slice! T or F: You're currently snuggling with a vegetarian.

Zucchini, Ricotta & Tarragon Tart

PREP TIME: 2 HOURS 30 MINUTES / TOTAL TIME: 4 HOURS / SERVINGS: 6-8

CRUST:

2 c all-purpose flour

1 t kosher salt

½ c olive oil, chilled in the freezer for 1 hour (it should be thick but pourable and still loose enough to stir)

6 T ice water

FILLING:

2 T olive oil

3 yellow onions, sliced into ½-inch disks

1 T champagne vinegar

Salt and pepper

2 medium zucchini, sliced into ¼-inch disks

½ c ricotta cheese

3 green tomatoes, sliced into ¼-inch disks and lightly salted

½ t finely chopped fresh tarragon

TO MAKE THE CRUST: Combine the flour and salt in a large food processor. Add the semi-frozen olive oil and blend. Add the ice water 1 tablespoon at a time with the motor running until a dough has formed. You're looking for a solid dough that holds together but isn't too sticky. You may need to adjust the amount of water due to factors like weather, altitude, moon cycle, etc. (maybe not moon cycle, but it's easy to blame that for things since we're all in touch with our inner werewolf). Remove the dough from the processor and form it into a big disk. Wrap it in plastic and refrigerate for at least an hour.

TO MAKE THE TART: Heat 1 tablespoon olive oil on medium heat in a large skillet. Add the yellow onions and cook until caramelized, about 30 minutes. Add the champagne vinegar, season with salt and pepper, and stir to mix well. Remove from the heat, transfer to a bowl, and set aside. Heat the remaining 1 tablespoon olive oil on medium-high heat in the same skillet. Add the zucchini and season with salt. Cook for about 10 minutes. Remove from the heat and set aside. Preheat the oven to 375°F. Spray a 12-inch tart pan with a removable bottom with cooking spray. Remove the dough from the fridge and place in the pan. Using your fingers, push the dough around and up the edge of the pan until it covers the entire pan evenly. Spread the ricotta on the bottom of the tart crust, then add the onions in an even layer. Layer the zucchini on top, slightly overlapping the slices, then arrange the green tomatoes on top in any fashion you like. Sprinkle with salt. Bake the tart in the oven for 30 minutes. Remove, let cool, sprinkle the chopped tarragon on top, and slice! T or F: Your vegetarian friends are moving in?

Eggplant, Feta & Basil Tart

PREP TIME: 2 HOURS 30 MINUTES / TOTAL TIME: 4 HOURS / SERVINGS: 6-8

CRUST:

2 c all-purpose flour

1 t kosher salt

½ c olive oil, chilled in the freezer for 1 hour (it should be thick but pourable and still loose enough to stir)

6 T ice water

FILLING:

2 medium eggplant, peeled and sliced into ¼-inch disks

SWOOPS

1 T olive oil

3 red onions, sliced into ½-inch disks

1 T balsamic vinegar

Salt and pepper

½ c feta cheese

3 heirloom tomatoes, sliced into ¼-inch disks and lightly salted

½ t finely chopped fresh basil

TO MAKE THE CRUST: Combine the flour and salt in a large food processor. Add the semi-frozen olive oil and blend. Add the ice water 1 tablespoon at a time with the motor running until a dough has formed. You're looking for a solid dough that holds together but isn't too sticky. You may need to adjust the amount of water due to factors like weather, altitude, political climate, etc. (maybe not political climate, but it's easy to blame that for things. Can I get an "Amen"?). Remove the dough from the processor and form it into a big disk. Wrap it in plastic and refrigerate for at least an hour.

TO MAKE THE TART: Preheat the oven to 375°F. Line a baking sheet with foil. Place the eggplant on the sheet and SWOOPS liberally. Bake for 30 minutes, or until starting to brown. Set aside. Meanwhile, heat the olive oil on medium heat in a large skillet. Add the red onions and cook until caramelized, about 30 minutes. Add the balsamic vinegar, season with salt and pepper, and stir to mix well. Remove from the heat and set aside. Spray a 12-inch tart pan with a removable bottom with cooking spray. Remove the dough from the fridge and place in the pan. Using your fingers, push the dough around and up the edge of the pan until it covers the entire pan evenly. Distribute the feta evenly on the bottom of the tart crust, then add the red onions in an even layer. Layer the eggplant on top, slightly overlapping the slices, then arrange the heirloom tomatoes on top. (Option: Arrange them in a big "J" for Jordan—just a suggestion.) Sprinkle with salt. Bake the tart in the oven for 30 minutes. Remove, let cool, sprinkle the chopped basil on top, and slice! T or F: There's a line of vegetarians knocking on your door?

CHEF'S LAGNIAPPE LESSON: A few years ago, I encountered a recipe that involved a peeled eggplant and it changed my life. I'm not being overly dramatic. Maybe the change wasn't as monumental as getting a dog or going to New Orleans for the first time, but it was certainly up there with getting a 3' phone charger cable so I don't have to hang halfway off my bed to use it while it's charging (thank you, ex-live-in gay*, for the lagniappe). I now compare it to peeling a potato; sometimes we like it dirty with the skins and sometimes we like it pristine and they're not missed.

* see page 88 for ex-live-in gay

WINE: **Sauvignon Blanc**
PRODUCER: **Mulderbosch**
REGION: **Stellenbosch, South Africa**
This dish will go well with a fine, aromatic white like Sauvignon Blanc, which offers intense aromas and flavors without any trace of oak. Mulderbosch, from the Stellenbosch region in South Africa, is well known as one of the finest Sauvignon Blanc producers in the world. We visited the Mulderbosch winery on a family trip to South Africa. I literally had just landed that morning after back-to-back red-eyes when I met my folks, who had arrived a few days earlier. They took me straight to the winery, and I fell asleep in the gift shop three tastings later. Jet lag is no joke. Have some afternoon dreams of your own of this recipe trifecta, accidental public snoozing at your own risk.

OPP: **Buitenverwachting, Bayten, Simonsig**

BAND: **Mofro**
ALBUM: *Lochloosa*
YEAR/GENRE: **(2004), Southern Rock**
I could listen to JJ Grey sing all summer long! Which works out because that's about how long it takes to make this masterpiece. Dirty, swampy Southern blues—I'm never not in the mood for it. JJ drips with musicality. You really haven't lived until you hear him sing. His voice, sweet and burnt like a great bourbon, resonates in your soul. "Mofro" was an old nickname of JJ's and he thought it explained the sound of the band better than "southern bluesy rock." One of my favorite memories from the much-missed Langerado music fest was rolling in Gracie's champagne Cadillac to the Mofro aftershow.

Mushroom,
Goat Cheese
& Thyme Tart

Mushroom, Goat Cheese & Thyme Tart

PREP TIME: 2 HOURS 30 MINUTES / TOTAL TIME: 4 HOURS / SERVINGS: 6-8

....

CRUST:

2 c all-purpose flour

1 t kosher salt

½ c olive oil, chilled in the freezer for 1 hour (it should be thick but pourable and still loose enough to stir)

6 T ice water

FILLING:

2 T olive oil

4 medium shallots, sliced into ½-inch disks

1 T red wine vinegar

½ t finely chopped fresh thyme

Salt and pepper

1 lb. mixed mushrooms

SWOOPS

4 Roma tomatoes, sliced into ¼-inch disks and lightly salted

½ c goat cheese

....

TO MAKE THE CRUST: Combine the flour and salt in a large food processor. Add the semi-frozen olive oil and blend. Add the ice water 1 tablespoon at a time with the motor running until a dough has formed. You're looking for a solid dough that holds together but isn't too sticky. You may need to adjust the amount of water due to factors like weather, altitude, social media algorithms, etc. (maybe not the algorithms, but it's easy to blame them for things. Who's with me?). Remove the dough from the processor and form it into a big disk. Wrap it in plastic and refrigerate for at least an hour.

TO MAKE THE TART: Heat 1 tablespoon olive oil on medium heat in a large skillet. Add the shallots and cook until caramelized, about 20 minutes. Add the red wine vinegar and thyme, season with salt and pepper, and stir to mix well. Remove from the heat, transfer to a bowl, and set aside. Heat the remaining 1 tablespoon olive oil on medium-high heat in the same skillet and add the mushrooms. Sauté for about 10 minutes, or until they've absorbed the oil and released their juices. SWOOPS. Preheat the oven to 375°F. Spray a 12-inch tart pan with a removable bottom with cooking spray. Remove the dough from the fridge and place in the pan. Using your fingers, push the dough around and up the edge of the pan until it covers the entire pan evenly. Distribute the goat cheese evenly on the bottom of the tart crust, then add the shallots in an even layer. Top with the mushrooms in an even layer, then arrange the Roma tomatoes on top, perhaps in a smiley face shape. Sprinkle with salt. Bake the tart in the oven for 30 minutes. Remove, let cool, and slice! T or F: The dog doesn't want to eat his/her chicken tonight?

WINE: **Tempranillo**
PRODUCER: **Bodegas Arzuaga Navarro**
REGION: **Ribera del Duero, Spain**

America is starting to notice Spain for its wealth of wine contributions. Though restaurants will tell you that diners predominantly order wines from France, Italy, and the U.S., Spain is starting to get added to that mix. Finally! Ribera del Duero is in northern Spain, located along the Duero River, and it has some of the highest vineyards in Spain to the tune of over 3,000 feet above sea level. These vines struggle at such a high elevation, which lends to the rich and concentrated character of the wine. A well-balanced, earthy Tempranillo from this region, where it is known as Tinto Fino, will pair well with this tart.

OPP: **Vega Sicilia 'Unico,' Emilio Moro, Viña Sastre**

ALBUM: **Merl Saunders and Jerry Garcia**
ALBUM: *Keystone Companions*
YEAR/GENRE: **(1973), Jam Rock**

Put on your red dress (also wine), baby. You're going out tonight, as the "Hi Heel Sneakers" album opener tells you. There was no way I wasn't going to find the right dish in this book to pair with this album. It's a guaranteed good time. Jerry and Merl played an eff-ton of shows together in the early '70s when the Dead weren't on the road, and this two-night stand from '73 was definitely the "Keepers." These shows encapsulate why fans loved them so much: A simple quartet configuration that sees the band running through a myriad of covers from blues, jazz, and R&B, often in long, languid takes that still keep your toes tapping. My baby girl name is Garcia. Jerry gets credit, but the nickname, Garcie, is also an anagram of my maternal grandmother, Gracie. Don't steal it—you're not my Rachel from "Friends."

SALADS

"The harmonicas play the skeleton keys and the rain
And these visions of Johanna are now all that remain"
— *Bob Dylan "Visions of Johanna"*

CROUTON-FREE CAESAR SALAD

We're not big on croutons in my family. They're dry, tasteless, and a waste of calories in our opinion. Here are four versions of a Caesar salad where I don't think you'll miss them much. Sure, ditching the croutons is an unconventional approach, but it makes the salad the star instead of merely a vessel for a heavy, goopy dressing or a substitute cheese cracker (you know this is what a Caesar turns into all too often).

WINE: Cabernet Sauvignon
PRODUCER: Stag's Leap
REGION: Napa Valley, CA
Not to be confused with its lesser imposter, Stags' Leap! (Mind your apostrophes!) We are getting a bit heartier with this winter dish, and that calls for a Napa Valley Cabernet Sauvignon. In 1976, there was this little competition called The Judgment of Paris, which pitted California wineries against world-renowned Burgundy and Bordeaux estates. You may have seen the movie *Bottleshock*, which showcased the winery that won the blind tasting of Chardonnays, Napa's Château Montelena. There was also a huge blind tasting of Cabernets and the 1973 Stag's Leap 'S.L.V.' won! So, it could be argued that Stag's Leap is a First Growth vineyard for Napa Valley.

OPP: Dunn Vineyards, Spottswoode, Mayacamas

BAND: The Greatest Showman
ALBUM: *Soundtrack*
YEAR/GENRE: (2017), Pop/Show Tunes
I watched this movie on an airplane, which never does a movie justice, and I still wound up in baggage claim singing the songs aloud. Obviously. What did you expect? "This Is Me." My quota for Broadway always has room for more, so when the multi-talented Hugh Jackman as P.T. Barnum boomed through the screen I was flying through the air with the greatest of ease and bonding with him from one ringleader to another. There's "Never Enough" of this Stag's Leap Cab when my dad opens a bottle. Make this salad once and you'll make it every winter, "From Now On."

Blue Cheese Caesar with Pear "Croutons"

PREP TIME: 30 MINUTES / TOTAL TIME: 45 MINUTES / SERVINGS: 6

2 anchovy fillets, finely chopped

¼ c grated Parmesan cheese

2 T fresh lemon juice (about ½ lemon)

2 t Dijon mustard

1 t finely chopped garlic (about 1 small clove)

½ t Worcestershire sauce

½ t hot sauce (my favorite is Crystal)

Salt and pepper

2 T full-fat plain Greek yogurt

½ c olive oil

2 hearts romaine lettuce

2 pears, cut into 1-inch cubes

½ c blue cheese crumbles

To make the dressing, combine the anchovies, Parmesan, lemon juice, mustard, garlic, Worcestershire sauce, hot sauce, ½ teaspoon salt, and ¼ teaspoon pepper in a small bowl and thoroughly mix together. Stir in the yogurt. (Put down the glass of Cab.) Slowly drizzle in the olive oil while constantly stirring (one hand pours, the other hand stirs) until it's fully incorporated into the dressing.

Cut off and discard the root ends of the romaine hearts. Chop the leaves into 1-inch pieces, wash, spin, and add to a large bowl. Sprinkle the pears and blue cheese on top. Add the dressing. Toss, too-us, 2-Us! ;-)

Tomato Caesar with Bacon "Croutons"

PREP TIME: 15 MINUTES / TOTAL TIME: 1 HOUR 15 MINUTES / SERVINGS: 6

2 c (about 1-pint carton) cherry tomatoes, halved (see 🥓 page 48) SWOOPS

2 eggs

4 bacon strips

2 anchovy fillets, finely chopped

¼ c grated Parmesan cheese

2 T fresh lemon juice, plus more for squeezing (about 1 lemon)

2 t Dijon mustard

1 t finely chopped garlic (about 1 small clove)

½ t Worcestershire sauce

½ t hot sauce (my favorite is Crystal)

Salt and pepper

2 T full-fat plain Greek yogurt

½ c olive oil

2 hearts romaine lettuce

Preheat the oven to 275°F.

Place the cherry tomatoes on a foil-lined tray, cut side up. SWOOPS. Roast in the oven for about an hour, until the tomatoes are slightly shriveled but not dried out—like they've been swimming, not like they've died. Remove from the oven and let cool.

Place the eggs in a small pot and fill with enough cold water to cover them by ½ inch. Bring to a boil. Reduce the heat to low and simmer for about 8 minutes (cooking time varies depending on altitude, weather, star alignment, and other thoroughly proven sciences). Remove the eggs from the pot and run them under cold water. Peel off the shell (an art in itself—I think my dog is better at this than I am), then slice the eggs in half and remove the yolks. Chop the egg whites, squeeze some lemon juice (from half of a lemon) on them, SWOOPS, and set aside.

Set the bacon strips in a large skillet over medium-high heat. Cook for 5 to 6 minutes per side, until golden brown and crispy. Drain on a paper towel-lined plate and let cool. Crumble the bacon into tiny bits and set aside.

To make the dressing, combine the anchovies, Parmesan, 2 tablespoons lemon juice, the mustard, garlic, Worcestershire sauce, hot sauce, ½ teaspoon salt, and ¼ teaspoon pepper in a small bowl and thoroughly mix together. Stir in the yogurt. (Put down the glass of Syrah.) Slowly drizzle in the olive oil while constantly stirring (one hand pours, the other hand stirs) until it's fully incorporated into the dressing.

Cut off and discard the root ends of the romaine hearts. Chop the leaves into 1-inch pieces, wash, spin, and add to a large bowl. Sprinkle the tomatoes, eggs, and bacon on top. Add the dressing. Toss, too-us, 2-Us! ;-)

PAIRINGS • WINE + MUSIC

WINE: **Syrah**
PRODUCER: **La Clarine Farm**
REGION: **Sierra Foothills, CA**
It's interesting how a person can despise cigarettes to such an extreme and yet gravitate toward everything else smoky. A fireplace burning on a dark, cold night, a campfire crackling lakeside, a Syrah seemingly dripping with char. Two hours south of Tahoe sits this natural winery, with high-altitude, cooler-climate vineyards that highlight the smoky characteristics of Syrah, that pair perfectly with bacon. I brought this wine to a spring, beachside lesbian wedding where one of the brides was Skyping in her family from Mexico. There were maybe eight people there, and we were swigging this from the bottle to make it feel like a proper beach bonfire. *Salud!*

OPP: **Haarmeyer, Terre Rouge**

BAND: **David Bowie**
ALBUM: *The Rise and Fall of Ziggy Stardust*
YEAR/GENRE: **(1972), Glam Rock**
A dressed-up album for a dressed-up, smoky, "Moonage Daydream" of a salad. What an album front to back! I did see Phish cover this album as their 2017 Halloween set in Vegas, thank you for asking. The arc of Bowie's career, morphing his style and look to each decade while still remaining unflappably himself, renders him a legendary visionary. Space age and flamboyant, *Ziggy Stardust* has got new edge for the season of newness. Also, Ziggy is my baby boy name. Ziggy Zucker, specifically.

Roasted Corn Caesar
with Squash "Croutons"

Roasted Corn Caesar with Squash "Croutons"

PREP TIME: 30 MINUTES / TOTAL TIME: 1 HOUR / SERVINGS: 6

1 yellow summer squash, cut into 1-inch cubes

1 zucchini, cut into 1-inch cubes

SWOOPS

2 ears corn

2 anchovy fillets, finely chopped

¼ c grated Parmesan cheese

2 T lemon juice (about ½ lemon)

2 t Dijon mustard

1 t finely chopped garlic (about 1 small clove)

½ t Worcestershire sauce

½ t hot sauce (my favorite is Crystal)

Salt and pepper

2 T full-fat plain Greek yogurt

½ c olive oil

2 hearts romaine lettuce

1 avocado

¼ c chopped fresh parsley

Heat a grill on high. Place both types of squash cubes (summer and zucchini) in a small bowl. SWOOPS. Grill the squash cubes, turning every few minutes, until lightly charred on all six sides. SWOOPS the ears of corn and grill, rolling, until charred all the way around. Remove from the grill and cut the corn kernels off the cob. Set aside.

To make the dressing, combine the anchovies, Parmesan, lemon juice, mustard, garlic, Worcestershire sauce, hot sauce, ½ teaspoon salt, and ¼ teaspoon pepper in a small bowl and thoroughly mix together. Stir in the yogurt. (Put down the glass of Albariño.) Slowly drizzle in the olive oil while constantly stirring (one hand pours, the other hand stirs) until it's fully incorporated into the dressing.

Cut off and discard the root ends of the romaine hearts. Chop the leaves into 1-inch pieces, wash, spin, and add to a large bowl. Halve, pit, and dice the avocado. Sprinkle the squash, zucchini, corn, avocado, and parsley on top. Add the dressing. Toss, too-us, 2-Us! ;-)

WINTER   SPRING   **SUMMER**   FALL

PAIRINGS · WINE + MUSIC

WINE: **Albariño**
PRODUCER: **Mar de Frades**
REGION: **Rías Baixas, Spain**
Me gusta Albariño! Dame más! (I like Albariño! Give me more!) Albariño and summer go together like peaches and cream. This one is from the Arousa estuary in the Rías Baixas region of northwest Spain, which sits on the Atlantic coast and specializes in crisp, zesty Albariño wines. Peachy keen. There isn't any oak here on this "Sea of Friars" Albariño. This wine is salty, briny, and sexy...what else did monks and friars have to pour their love and desire into other than making beautiful wines?

OPP: **Palacio de Fefiñes, Zarate, Pazo de Señorans**

BAND: **Armik**
ALBUM: *Rosas de Amor*
YEAR/GENRE: **(1987), Flamenco**
Some Spanish guitar with your Spanish Albariño. This one is all thanks to Jim. (Thanks, Dad!) I was up at our place in Vermont with four friends for our night off between Phish concerts. We had put a CD in an empty slot in my dad's 300-disc carousel (raise your hand if your folks still use a disc carousel), which then went on to play the next disc which already lived there: Hello, *Rosas de Amor*! We sat outside in the warm New England summer evening, guzzling wine (likely an Albariño if I'm doing my job right) and relaxing to this album. Everyone returned home with a padded music repertoire. Turns out, our Armik was a child prodigy who, at seven, pawned his watch for a classical guitar and hid in the basement to practice. Thirty-six solo albums later, the dude is a Nuevo flamenco legend. He uses 12 different guitars on this album, about as many varieties of ingredients in the dish!

WINE: **Fer Servadou**
PRODUCER: **Nicolas Carmarans 'Fer de Sang' Rouge**
REGION: **Aveyron, France**
This is one of my wines from Lou* Amdur at his eponymous shop in Los Feliz. I always go to Lou to stock up for a party or an event. All of his wines will be special, interesting, and compatible with a range of budgets. This one from southwestern France is light enough for a simple salad and peppery enough to complement this Caesar version. Another biodynamic wine! The local Fer Servadou grape, which is light and thin-skinned, sees 10 days of carbonic maceration, enhancing its peppy fruit and lift. This one is a delight, created with care and no compromise or cutting corners.

*Other wines from Lou; see pages 68 & 148

OPP: **L'Enclos des Braves, Domaine Plageoles, Domaine du Cros 'Marcillac'**

BAND: **Dr. Dog**
ALBUM: *Be the Void*
YEAR/GENRE: **(2012), Indie Rock**
Dr. Dog's blend of psychedelia and indie sound emulates the peppers and polenta of this dish. When I was working hospitality at the High Sierra Music Fest one year, Dr. Dog was headlining the stage where I was stationed, but I had that shift off. After an interesting and memorable combination of main-stage pit access rejection and failed attempt to meet up with friends, I returned to the Dr. Dog stage solo and watched the entire set side stage in awe and glory. They were my heroes of the night, and I've been in love with them ever since. A heady but quirky indie rock band, they wear their late '60s influences proudly on their hipster sleeves. So tight, so good!

Roasted Pepper Caesar with Polenta "Croutons"

PREP TIME: 1 HOUR / TOTAL TIME: 1 HOUR 30 MINUTES / SERVINGS: 6

SWOOPS

2 red bell peppers

1 c chicken stock

1 c cornmeal

Salt and pepper

½ c plus 2 T olive oil

2 anchovy fillets, finely chopped

½ c grated Parmesan cheese

2 T lemon juice (about ½ lemon)

2 t Dijon mustard

1 t finely chopped garlic (about 1 small clove)

½ t Worcestershire sauce

½ t hot sauce (my favorite is Crystal)

2 T full-fat plain Greek yogurt

2 hearts romaine lettuce

¼ c capers

Preheat the oven to 450°F.

SWOOPS the red peppers. Place on a foil-lined baking sheet and roast for about 40 minutes, rotating every so often, until charred on all sides. Once roasted, remove from the oven and place in a brown paper bag to let cool for about 20 minutes. Peel away the skins and wash away the seeds so that you're left with just the roasted flesh. Chop, SWOOPS, and set aside.

Meanwhile, heat the chicken stock in a medium saucepan on medium-high. Add the cornmeal and stir. Season with salt and pepper. Bring to a boil, then reduce the heat to low and simmer, stirring constantly, until the polenta is cooked, about 20 minutes. It'll look like porridge and all the liquid will be incorporated into the cornmeal. Not too soupy, not too dry and goopy, but juuuust right and pourable, Goldilocks!

Spray a baking sheet with nonstick cooking spray. Pour the polenta onto the sheet and spread into an even layer. Refrigerate for about an hour, until the polenta has solidified and doesn't jiggle. Cut the polenta into 1-inch cubes. Heat 2 tablespoons olive oil in a medium skillet on medium-high, add the polenta "croutons" (in batches, if necessary), and sauté until browned and crispy on all sides. If they're falling apart, try patting them dry first before sending them to the scorcher. Drain and set aside.

To make the dressing, combine the anchovies, ¼ cup Parmesan, the lemon juice, mustard, garlic, Worcestershire sauce, hot sauce, ½ teaspoon salt, and ¼ teaspoon pepper in a small bowl and thoroughly mix together. Stir in the yogurt. (Put down the glass of Fer Servadou—also known as Braucol and Mansois in other regions.) Slowly drizzle in the remaining ½ cup olive oil while constantly stirring (one hand pours, the other hand stirs) until it's fully incorporated into the dressing.

Cut each romaine heart lengthwise. SWOOPS the cut side. Heat a grill pan to medium-high and spray with nonstick cooking spray. Grill the romaine for 1 to 2 minutes, until charred. Remove from the pan and chop. Place the romaine on a serving tray. Throw the roasted peppers, polenta "croutons," capers, and remaining ¼ cup Parmesan on top. Drizzle with the dressing.

GRILLED FRUIT SALAD

I made my Grilled Watermelon Salad when I guest-starred on *Grill It! with Bobby Flay* on the Food Network. A great red wine vinaigrette combined with the flavors of mint, coconut, and feta goes well with many fruits you can find at the market any time of year. The secret weapon is using homemade red wine vinegar (see  page 82).

WINE: Sparkling
PRODUCER: Philippe Foreau Vouvray Brut
REGION: Touraine, Loire Valley, France
Who doesn't like to lean on the sparkles in the winter? I really like this Vouvray. It'll have you celebrating tropical thoughts while you indulge in this colada-daiquiri-inspired salad. This sparkling wine goes the extra mile and spends four years on lees prior to disgorgement—which is two years longer than the minimum required for Champagne. Chenin Blanc is the only grape allowed to grow in Vouvray. Although Vouvray is a small region in the Loire Valley, it boasts a vast variety of sweetness levels in both still and sparkling wines. Chenin Blanc is one of the most acidic varieties out there, so just like with Rieslings, oftentimes there is residual sugar to balance out the final product.

OPP: Champalou, François Pinon, Domaine Huet

BAND: The Word
ALBUM: The Word
YEAR/GENRE: (2001), Blues Rock
The Word is a supergroup comprised of Luther, Cody, and Chris from The North Mississippi Allstars on guitar, drums, and bass, Robert Randolph on pedal steel, and John Medeski on keys. When they were first touring, I saw their show at House of Blues for my birthday. (I practically lived there in my 20s; there's a hole in my soul now that it's been leveled.) While they've only periodically toured—most recently in 2015—here's to hoping to see more of them soon! So enjoy the "Joyful Sounds" of Vouvray popping and fizzing while you add some sparkle to your winter day.

Grilled Pineapple & Banana Salad

PREP TIME: 30 MINUTES / TOTAL TIME: 45 MINUTES / SERVINGS: 6(-ISH)

SWOOPS

1 pineapple, peeled and sliced

1 banana, peeled and sliced

2 blood oranges, peeled, sectioned, and pulled into 1-inch pieces

1 c chopped fresh coconut

½ c crumbled feta cheese

½ c olive oil

2 T red wine vinegar

1 T chopped sweet onion

1 t vanilla salt (If you can't find it at the market, make your own by throwing a split fresh vanilla bean into a bowl of salt to infuse it.)

½ t cayenne pepper

1 c chopped fresh mint

Heat a grill on high. SWOOPS the pineapple slices and put them on the grill for a few minutes until they get nice char marks. Flip and repeat, then transfer to a cutting board and chop. If it looks like there's some pineapple missing, it's probably because you ate it plain. This is allowed. Put the surviving chopped grilled pineapple in a large bowl and add the banana, blood oranges, coconut, and crumbled feta. In a smaller bowl, whisk together the olive oil, vinegar, onion, vanilla salt, and cayenne to combine. Pour over the fruit mixture, add the mint, and toss, too-us away!

CHEF'S LAGNIAPPE LESSON: Homemade red wine vinegar can be a total game changer, and making it is so easy if you have three basic pieces of equipment: 1) an uncharred barrel—any uncharred wood aging barrel (likely oak) will do. A 5-liter barrel lives on my bar; 2) a mother—this is the fermenting agent that turns the alcohol into acid, resulting in the taste change from wine to vinegar; and 3) leftover red wine that you like to drink—the key to good vinegar is that you have to start with good wine. Once a bottle of red is opened, it has a limited shelf life before it oxidizes and turns. Remains of the bottle are the perfect candidate for the vinegar base. Just use a funnel to pour the wine into the barrel and let the mother work its magic.

CHEF'S LAGNIAPPE LESSON: I personally use red wine vinegar sparingly in my kitchen. This has proved to be a convenient practice because the amount of leftover wine in my house has significantly decreased since the advent of the Coravin—a wine preservation opener and a single girl's best friend. It's not quite as useful as a boyfriend with whom to share the bottle, and, with its clumsy mechanics, it's about as sexy as a chastity belt, but it does allow you to access the wine without uncorking the bottle, meaning it will stay good for weeks. The RWV barrel still gets its fill with the leftover wine after a good party.

Grilled Mango & Strawberry Salad

PREP TIME: 30 MINUTES / TOTAL TIME: 45 MINUTES / SERVINGS: 6(-ISH)

SWOOPS

2 mangoes, peeled and sliced

12 oz. (1-pint carton) strawberries, stemmed and halved vertically (see 🧆 page 48)

1 c chopped fresh coconut

½ c crumbled feta cheese

½ c olive oil

2 T red wine vinegar (see 🧆 page 82)

1 T chopped sweet onion

1 t vanilla salt (If you can't find it at the market, make your own by throwing a split fresh vanilla bean into a bowl of salt to infuse it.)

½ t cayenne pepper

1 c chopped fresh mint

Heat a grill on high. SWOOPS the mango slices and put them on the grill for a few minutes until they get nice char marks. Flip and repeat, then transfer to a cutting board and chop. If it looks like you have less mango than you started with, it's probably because you ate it. I support this. Put the surviving chopped grilled mango in a large bowl and add the strawberries, coconut, and crumbled feta. In a smaller bowl, whisk together the olive oil, vinegar, onion, vanilla salt, and cayenne to combine. Pour over the fruit mixture, add the mint, and toss, too-us away!

CHEF'S LAGNIAPPE LESSON: Mangoes are a huge pain in the ass. It's not you, it's them. They are my biggest produce lament, just as artichokes are for my mom. I try to peel them and then slice as much flesh off of the big, flat pit in the middle as possible, but this is tricky because the mangoes will slip and slide all over the damn cutting board. I have the most success when I leave the skin on and cut off big chunks from the pit, then peel the slices, as opposed to peeling first and then cutting slippery flesh off the pit. That said, they are well worth the work and wait. So are the artichokes.

WINE: **White Blend**
PRODUCER: **Channing Daughters 'Cuvee Tropical'**
REGION: **Long Island, NY**
Channing Daughters is my favorite of the South Fork of Long Island wineries and a routine stop during any Hamptons weekend. This one will match the tropical notes of the fruit salad to enhance your "Calgon, take me away" experience with every bite and sip. This wine blasts out of the glass with Chardonnay and Muscat. The Muscat grape is very aromatic and has a beautiful aroma of lychee and honeysuckle. The Chardonnay provides the backbone and structure to this blend. I would save this salad and wine for a patio on a hot summer day.

OPP: **Lieb Family Cellars 'Bridge Lane,' Wölffer Estate, Macari**

BAND: **Tom Petty**
ALBUM: **Wildflowers**
YEAR/GENRE: **(1994), Rock**
I've repeatedly made the mistake of letting my mother set me up on dates. One of the most massive disasters was when one guy was coming down from San Francisco to visit/meet me. I popped in this album and we headed up to Santa Barbara to see Tom Petty at the Bowl (despite my "no listening to the band we're going to see on the way to/from the show" rule). Let's just say that Tom Petty was the best part of the evening. The whole night is worthy of a book of its own. This ranks as one of my favorite driving albums of all time too. So roll down the window, breathe in those spring wildflowers, and enjoy the sweet vibrancy of the fruit of Petty's labor.

WINE: **Rosé**
PRODUCER: **Wagner-Stempel**
REGION: **Rheinhessen, Germany**

Some watermelon-colored juice to go with the watermelon salad. This one is easy drinking, a "rosé all day" crowd-pleaser. It's probably my current favorite. This winery has been family owned now for nine generations. This particular wine is comprised of Pinot Noir and St. Laurent (an indigenous grape to Austria). This wine is dry and invigorating, which allows the watermelon to take on the sweetness spotlight, but also refuses to be ignored.

OPP: **Künstler, von Winning, Leitz**

BAND: **Herbie Hancock**
ALBUM: *Takin' Off*
YEAR/GENRE: **(1962), Jazz, Hard Bop**

Some "Watermelon Man" with your watermelon salad. One of the most stunning debuts in jazz that also features all original compositions—with Dexter Gordon (sax) and Freddie Hubbard (trumpet) supporting—Herbie revisited "Watermelon Man" a decade later on his space-funk masterpiece *Headhunters*. The latter version has been sampled by everyone from Diggable Planets to Madonna on the oft-overlooked *Bedtime Stories*. Maybe if you eat, sip, and listen in the right amounts at the right time, you can channel some of Herbie's fountain of youth. We marvel every year when he plays a birthday show at the Hollywood Bowl. He officially has fewer wrinkles than I do (though some days I fear my bulldog can claim the same...).

Grilled Watermelon & Raspberry Salad

PREP TIME: 30 MINUTES   /   TOTAL TIME: 45 MINUTES   /   SERVINGS: 6(-ISH)

SWOOPS

1 (5-lb.) watermelon, cut in half and sliced

2 c (two ½-pint cartons) raspberries (see 🥄 page 48)

1 c chopped fresh coconut

½ c crumbled feta cheese

½ c olive oil

2 T red wine vinegar (see 🥄 page 82)

1 T chopped sweet onion

1 t vanilla salt (If you can't find it at the market, make your own by throwing a split fresh vanilla bean into a bowl of salt to infuse it.)

½ t cayenne pepper

1 c chopped fresh mint

Heat a grill on high. SWOOPS the watermelon slices and put them on the grill for a few minutes until they get nice char marks. Flip and repeat, then transfer to a cutting board and chop. Pick at the grilled fruit and sneak a piece to the dog. Put the surviving chopped grilled watermelon into a large bowl and add the raspberries, coconut, and crumbled feta. In a smaller bowl, whisk together the olive oil, vinegar, onion, vanilla salt, and cayenne to combine. Pour over the fruit mixture, add the mint, and toss, too-us away! Turn on Food Network in case there's a Bobby Flay rerun on. (Spoiler alert: There's not.)

WINTER   SPRING   SUMMER   FALL

Grilled Watermelon Salad

WINE: **Falanghina**
PRODUCER: **Terredora di Paolo 'Irpinia'**
REGION: **Campania, Italy**

Terredora di Paolo is a family-run winery in Campania, in southern Italy. My first introduction to the Falanghina grape was at a restaurant where I got into an argument with the server because he pronounced it as if it rhymed with a female body part (Fah-luhn-JY-na). I was pretty certain the "h" made it a hard "g," and that phonetically in Italian it would rhyme with "arena." (Fah-luhn-GHEE-na) The server, of course, was completely disinterested in arriving at the truth. Even after we finished the bottle, it mattered to me. So mind your hard Gs, please—this wine deserves proper representation. The salty feta and the minerality component of this wine play perfectly together. And the sweetness of the plum magically enhances the wine's aromas.

OPP: **Fattoria La Rivolta, Quintodecimo, Feudi di San Gregorio**

BAND: **Steely Dan**
ALBUM: *Aja*
YEAR/GENRE: **(1977), Jazz Rock**

I remember the moment I stopped wanting to see live music with the hope of hearing album-like renditions and, rather, simply going to hear the music performed live by the musicians in real time. That year I went to see Steely Dan with a friend and she minorly griped that she didn't know any of the songs until the encore. I told her about my newfound concert outlook and she soon became one of my loyal Partners in Crime (PsIC) on the front rail at concerts, all thanks to hearing "Peg" for the first time live. As far as Yacht Rock masterpieces, *Aja* is near the top. Serve up some Falanghina with plums and your guests "I know will love you better."

Grilled Plum & Grape Salad

PREP TIME: 30 MINUTES / TOTAL TIME: 1 HOUR / SERVINGS: 6(-ISH)

....

4 plums
SWOOPS

1 c green grapes

1 c chopped fresh coconut

½ c crumbled feta cheese

½ c olive oil

2 T red wine vinegar (see page 82)

1 T chopped sweet onion

1 t vanilla salt (If you can't find it at the market, make your own by throwing a split fresh vanilla bean into a bowl of salt to infuse it.)

½ t cayenne pepper

1 c chopped fresh mint

....

Heat a grill on high. Slice the plums in half and remove the pits. SWOOPS the flesh of the plums and place them on the grill cut side down until they get nice char marks. Transfer to a cutting board and chop. Slice the grapes in half (tedious but worth it; if you don't expose the flesh it won't soak up the surrounding flavors. Same general rule for tomatoes or anything else with a nonporous skin). If you find some fruit missing, it's probably because your company has caught on to your ways. Put the surviving plums and grapes in a large bowl and add the coconut and crumbled feta. In a smaller bowl, whisk together the olive oil, vinegar, onion, vanilla salt, and cayenne to combine. Pour over the fruit mixture, add mint, and toss, too-us away!

Grilled Plum Salad

SPINACH SALAD
(with Jar Shaker Dressing)

My ex-live-in gays* will confirm that a top kitchen rule in my house is "No store-bought salad dressings."
There are so many chemicals and added fillers in most of them. And since they're so easy to make at home,
there's no reason to buy dressing. Go natural or bust! Seriously, I SMH (shake my head) and tsk (Turkish
noise for disapproval) just thinking of what to say and scoff at anything store-bought. But let's not overreact
here. If you're an emulsion stickler, then you'll probably go a different route than the jar shaker dressing.
For these salads, my mom and I really were tickled by the sautéed cucumbers as a nice twist.

*An ex-live-in gay is generally one (or two) of your best friends who has to move into your guest room and
live with you while he/she/they are "between homes/house-hunting/renovating" and the three of you live
in perfect harmony like an adorable family for a year. I recommend everyone have at least one at some point.

Apple, Cheddar
& Peanut Salad

Apple, Cheddar & Peanut Spinach Salad

PREP TIME: 30 MINUTES / TOTAL TIME: 1 HOUR / SERVINGS: 6

DRESSING:

3 T freshly squeezed blood orange juice

2 T balsamic vinegar

¼ c olive oil

Salt and pepper

SALAD:

1 T olive oil

1 shallot, chopped

1 leek, white and light green parts only, thinly sliced (see  page 37)

8 oz. (about 1 c) string beans, trimmed and halved

2 Persian cucumbers, cut into ½-inch disks

Salt and pepper

¼ c peanuts

1 apple (recommendation: Gala), cored and diced

1 (10-oz.) package prewashed baby spinach

¼ c shredded Cheddar cheese

TO MAKE THE DRESSING: In a jar, combine the blood orange juice, vinegar, and olive oil. Season with salt and pepper. Secure the lid to the jar. Shake, shake, shake! Make sure you re-shake, shake, shake at the last minute, right before dressing the salad. Shake your booty.

TO MAKE THE SALAD: Heat the olive oil in a large skillet over medium heat. Add the shallot and leek and cook until sweating, about 2 minutes. Add the string beans and cucumbers, season with salt and pepper, and toss! Continue cooking for 2 to 3 more minutes, until the string beans are al dente. Too-us! In a separate pan over medium heat, toast the peanuts for about 3 minutes, until fragrant. Be sure not to burn them (this usually happens when you've been standing there waiting for them to toast and then you leave the room for a quick second to check email or go to the bathroom, confident you'll be right back, and end up forgetting about them). Remove the nuts from the heat and chop. Add the apples to the sautéed veggies in the skillet, then transfer the mixture to a large bowl. Add half of the dressing and toss! Add the peanuts and too-us! Add the spinach and too-us! Add the Cheddar and too-us! I like to use tongs for all of this. Once everything is well coated, season to taste, adjust dressing level as desired, and serve!

CHEF'S LAGNIAPPE LESSON: Quick geography tutorial on Napa and Sonoma Valley. They are neighboring counties separated by the Mayacamas Mountains. Hence they're referred to both by County and Valley. Furthermore, they each seat a main downtown city each respectively called Napa and Sonoma. So the wines are often described more specifically to their AVAs—e.g., St. Helena, Napa or Healdsburg, Sonoma to distinguish between the towns, but still carry the prestige of the region.

WINE: **Cabernet Sauvignon**
PRODUCER: **Jordan Winery**
REGION: **Alexander Valley, Sonoma Valley, California**
I cleaned house in the gift shop at the Jordan Winery on yet another Napa/Sonoma bachelorette party. Since they're so close by, it's easy to hit both valleys in one weekend (See ). The Jordan Winery happened to be the stuffiest of the ones we visited, but they make a damn good Cab, and putting peanuts in your salad clears you from any pretentiousness. A big, rich Cabernet Sauvignon is a classic pairing with Cheddar cheese, hearty, leafy greens, and nut fats.

OPP: **Corison, Coppola, Banshee**

BAND: **Lou Reed**
ALBUM: *Transformer*
YEAR/GENRE: **(1972), Glam Rock**
Down that Jordan Cab and take a walk on the wild side. Lou's wistful voice just exudes the reserved emotions of winter to me. His second album post-Velvet Underground, he turned to the dynamic duo of David Bowie and Mick Ronson to co-produce, which helped break him to bigger European audiences. It manages to be austere but sumptuous, gaunt but hungry. At this point, Lou (along with Bowie) was in full glam mode, guy-liner applied as heavy as the Cab. With three timeless tunes that would define his career for the next 40 years—"Perfect Day," "Walk on the Wild Side," and "Satellite of Love"— this album feels like a Kennedy marrying a Soprano.

WINE: *Chardonnay*
PRODUCER: **Domaine Serene**
REGION: **Willamette Valley, OR**

Technically I am an ABC (Anything But Chard) person. I want no part of a buttery or oaky white. I prefer my whites to smack me a bit. When I went wine tasting in Willamette I was embarrassed about digging their Chards. I was so intent on drowning in the Pinots that put Willamette on the map, it took me by surprise. The Chardonnay from Domaine Serene is made with very little new oak (in line with the region's style) and is super crunchy. I'll drink it with pride. Family-owned Domaine Serene (named after the winemaker's daughter, Serene) has always been one of my favorite wineries (their Pinot Noirs are bomb diggity too!). The brightness of the Chardonnay plays well with the peas and has the acidity to cut through the sweetness of the strawberries.

OPP: **Gran Moraine, Walter Scott, Evening Land**

BAND: **Alanis Morissette**
ALBUM: *Jagged Little Pill*
YEAR/GENRE: **(1995), Alt Rock**

Listen to this one with your Chardonnay, no black fly. Alanis surprised consumers with a move away from her previous dance pop into something far more alternative sounding. Lead single "You Oughta Know" features Dave Navarro on guitar and Flea on bass while also containing such lyrical gems for modern rock radio. I, for one, can't go into a movie theater without hearing "an older version of me," etc. She gets a little dark (death row, plane crashes) and dated. (Are smoking breaks still a thing?) Ironically, the album holds up and you'll likely have one hand in your pocket and the other one catching a rogue pea.

Strawberry, Pea & Hazelnut Spinach Salad

PREP TIME: 30 MINUTES / TOTAL TIME: 1 HOUR / SERVINGS: 6

DRESSING:

3 T orange juice, freshly squeezed

2 T balsamic vinegar

¼ c olive oil

Salt and pepper

SALAD:

1 T olive oil

1 red onion, chopped

8 oz. (about 1 c) string beans, trimmed and halved horizontally

Salt and pepper

½ c baby peas (can be frozen)

¼ c hazelnuts

8 oz. strawberries, stemmed and sliced

1 (10-oz.) package prewashed baby spinach

¼ c blue cheese crumbles

TO MAKE THE DRESSING: In a jar, combine the orange juice, vinegar, and olive oil. Season with salt and pepper. Secure the lid to the jar. Shake, shake, shake! Make sure you re-shake, shake, shake at the last minute, right before dressing the salad. Like a Polaroid picture.

TO MAKE THE SALAD: Heat the olive oil in a large skillet over medium heat. Add the onion and cook until sweating, about 2 minutes. Add the string beans, season with salt and pepper, and toss! Continue cooking for 2 to 3 more minutes, until the string beans are al dente. Add the peas and cook for another minute, until warmed through.

In a separate pan over medium heat, toast the hazelnuts for about 1 minute, until fragrant. Be sure not to burn them (this can happen if you abandon the stove for what you're sure will be a 30-second score check but turns out to be longer). Add them to the skillet with the sautéed veggies and mix until the nuts are coated.

Transfer the mixture to a large bowl. Add half of the dressing and too-us! Add the strawberries and too-us! Add the spinach and toss! Add the blue cheese and too-us! I like to use tongs for all of this. Once everything is well coated, season to taste, adjust dressing level as desired, and serve!

Strawberry, Pea
& Hazelnut Salad

PAIRINGS · WINE + MUSIC

WINE: Grenache Blanc
PRODUCER: Uproot
REGION: Edna Valley, Central Coast, California
I discovered Uproot at a Wine Riot event. Being the sucker for marketing that I am, I was first intrigued by their color-coded labels, where each piece represents a different flavor element of the wine. All of their wines were top-notch. Uproot now teams up with Girls Guide, awarding wine packages to winners of our sports brackets! This unique and whimsical wine with flavors of peach and petrol pairs beautifully with the obvious nectarine and the sweet creaminess of the cashew, and successfully tempers the goat cheese funk.

OPP: Donkey & Goat, Tablas Creek Vineyard

BAND:
The Allman Brothers Band
ALBUM: *Eat a Peach*
YEAR/GENRE: (1972), Southern Rock
What's the difference between a nectarine and a peach? Well, they're practically identical genetically, but peaches have the fuzz and nectarines are smooth-skinned. Since they're so similar, they can often be used interchangeably, so go ahead and follow the Allmans' lead and eat a peach if that's more your jam! You'll have plenty of time to finish your bottle of Grenache Blanc during the 33-plus-minute "Mountain Jam." "Blue Sky" puts the G.O.A.T. in this salad too—IMO, it's the greatest Dickey Betts tune of all time. Take note of the "Little Martha" track because I reference it in another music pairing (see page 58).

Nectarine, Cashew & Goat Cheese Spinach Salad

PREP TIME: 30 MINUTES / TOTAL TIME: 1 HOUR / SERVINGS: 6

DRESSING:

3 T orange juice, freshly squeezed

2 T balsamic vinegar

¼ c olive oil

Salt and pepper

SALAD:

1 T olive oil

1 red onion, chopped

8 oz. (about 1 c) snow peas, trimmed and halved

2 Persian cucumbers, cut into ½-inch disks

Salt and pepper

¼ c cashews

2 nectarines, pitted, sliced into wedges, then chopped

1 (10-oz.) package prewashed baby spinach

¼ c goat cheese crumbles

¼ c purslane leaves

TO MAKE THE DRESSING: In a jar, combine the orange juice, vinegar, and olive oil. Season with salt and pepper. Secure the lid to the jar. Shake, shake, shake! Make sure you re-shake, shake, shake at the last minute, right before dressing the salad. Shake it up. Dance all night. Play all day.

TO MAKE THE SALAD: Heat the olive oil in a large skillet over medium heat. Add the onion and cook until sweating, about 2 minutes. Add the snow peas and cucumbers, season with salt and pepper, and too-us! Continue cooking for 2 to 3 more minutes, until the snow peas are al dente.

In a separate pan over medium heat, toast the cashews for about 3 minutes, until fragrant. Be sure not to burn them (this can happen if you get lost in a "Blue Sky" air guitar jam, but where's Dickey Betts to eat your burnt nuts now?!?!). Remove the nuts from the heat and chop. Add to the sautéed veggies in the skillet and mix until the nuts are coated.

Transfer the mixture to a large bowl. Add half of the dressing and toss! Add the nectarines and too-us! Add the spinach and toss! Add the goat cheese and too-us! I like to use tongs for all of this. Sprinkle the purslane leaves on top. Once everything is well coated, season to taste, adjust dressing level as desired, and serve!

WINTER   SPRING   SUMMER   FALL

Persimmon, Pepita & Pecorino Spinach Salad

PREP TIME: 30 MINUTES / TOTAL TIME: 1 HOUR / SERVINGS: 6

. . . .

DRESSING:

3 T orange juice, freshly squeezed

2 T balsamic vinegar

¼ c olive oil

Salt and pepper

SALAD:

1 T olive oil

1 red onion, chopped

2 Persian cucumbers, cut into ½-inch disks

Salt and pepper

¼ c pepitas, shelled

2 Hachiya persimmons, sliced

1 (10-oz.) package prewashed baby spinach

¼ c grated pecorino cheese

. . . .

TO MAKE THE DRESSING: In a jar, combine the orange juice, vinegar, and olive oil. Season with salt and pepper. Secure the lid to the jar. Shake, shake, shake! Make sure you re-shake, shake, shake at the last minute, right before dressing the salad. That's right, you got me shakin'.

TO MAKE THE SALAD: Heat the olive oil in a large skillet over medium heat. Add the onion and cook until sweating, about 2 minutes. Add the cucumbers, season with salt and pepper, and too-us! Continue cooking for about 2-3 more minutes (until al dente).

In a separate pan over medium heat, toast the pepitas for about 2 minutes, until fragrant. Be sure not to burn them (I set a timer because I personally can't be trusted to refrain from distraction. Wait, who's at the door?). Remove the pepitas from the heat and chop. Add to the sautéed veggies in the skillet and mix until the pepitas are coated.

Transfer the mixture to a large bowl. Add half of the dressing and toss! Add the persimmons and too-us! Add the spinach and too-us! Add the pecorino and too-us! I like to use tongs for all of this. Once everything is well coated, season to taste, adjust dressing level as desired, and serve!

WINE: **Grenache**
PRODUCER: **Mathis**
REGION: **Sonoma Valley, CA**
I died over this red, discovered at a restaurant in Sonoma, where, let's face it, we were likely celebrating yet another bachelorette party. (Side note: My bachelorette party will be in Bali.) I'll call it the Popeye find of the weekend. It's complex but fun, and packs enough punch with ripe fruit flavors to complement the salad—much like spinach does—but not too much to compete with the essential elements, making Olive Oyl swoon. Peter Mathis was the winemaker for Ravenswood for twenty years before starting up his eponymous passion project. Persimmon packs a motley combination of flavors and a somewhat odd texture profile of apple, mango, and tomato. Grenache is "everybody's buddy," so it tends to pair well with unique flavor and texture profiles.

OPP: **Dashe, Birichino, Bonny Doon**

BAND: **Bill Withers**
ALBUM: **Lean on Me: The Best of Bill Withers**
YEAR/GENRE: **(1994; music is from the '70s), Soul**
This album is seventies soul at its best. "Use Me," an all-time fave, led to one of my favorite NY moments ever. I had just seen *Any Given Sunday* with my parents on the Upper East Side. I wanted to like the movie more but said that I couldn't complain because of its big "Use Me" montage. A stranger who couldn't help but overhear my loudmouth review in the intersection of 86th and 3rd stopped mid crosswalk and challenged, "I'll give you ten bucks if you know who wrote that song." "Bill Withers!" I offered. He smiled, shook my hand, and reached into his wallet for my reward—which I obviously declined. The real reward is Bill's music on a fall day even when there "Ain't No Sunshine."

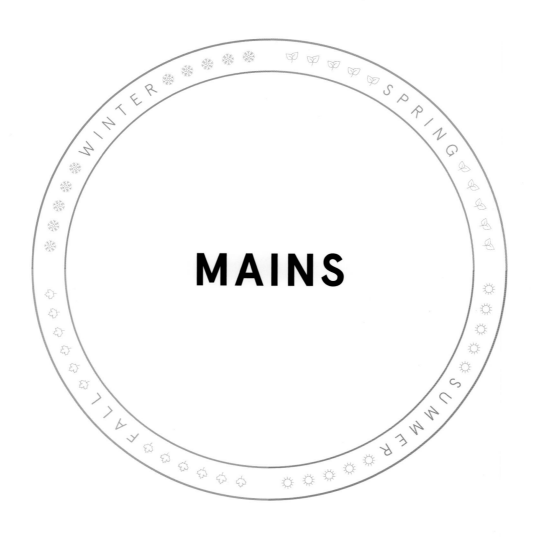

MAINS

FISH

Sunday is the West Hollywood Farmers' Market, and I traditionally go get a fish, a green, and a veggie to roast all together for dinner. The juices emitted from the fish help cook the bed of greens. Here are some of my favorite pairings throughout the year.

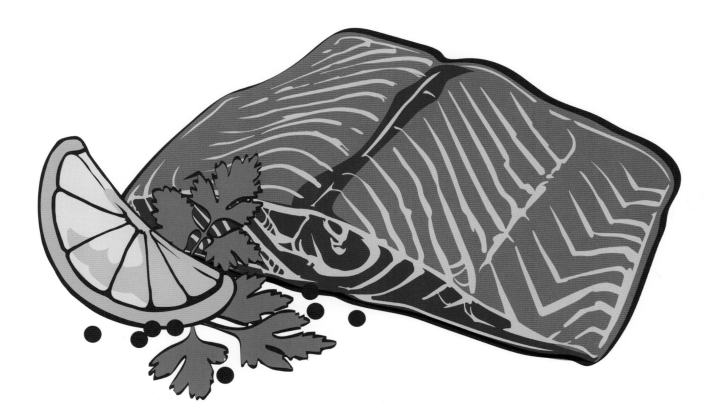

Smoky-Rub Salmon with Chard & Carrots

PREP TIME: 15 MINUTES / TOTAL TIME: 25 MINUTES / SERVINGS: 4

WINE: **Pinot Noir**
PRODUCER: **Rochioli**
REGION: **Russian River Valley, Sonoma Valley, CA**

There is no wine better suited for salmon than a Pinot Noir, and Russian River Pinot Noirs are world-class. This Rochioli was one of the first wines I remember fainting over as an adult. (By "adult," I mean an age when I took interest in keeping track of wines to shop for myself.) My dad was visiting me when I had freshly moved to L.A., and we both "ooh"ed and "aah"ed over it. We must have been extremely loud about it because it doubled in price the following vintage. Word's out! The single-vineyard estate wines of this winery are now for wine club members only and a five-year waiting list. So please stop telling everyone about this wine.

OPP: **Littorai, Kistler, Claypool Cellars, Capiaux**

BAND: **Jimmy McGriff**
ALBUM: *Electric Funk*
YEAR/GENRE: **(1970), Jazz Funk**

I discovered this jazz organist because someone had added a few of his songs to my iPod back in the day. (Remember when that was a thing to do for people?) I got hooked and dove deeper into his catalog. This features the punchy sax of Stanley Turrentine (who's also on Jimmy Smith's *Back at the Chicken Shack,* see page 105) and the immaculate groove of drummer Bernard Purdie. It'll keep you warm on a cold day along with some salmon and Pinot. (It may also be suitable for bedroom escapades, but that isn't in this book.) Also T or F: My Glyph external hard drive is named Jimmy McGlyph. (Hint: T or Fs are usually T in my circle of friends.)

---

1 bunch Swiss chard

SWOOPS

3 carrots, peeled and chopped into 1-inch pieces

1 T brown sugar

1 T ground cumin

1 T smoked paprika

1 t smoked salt

1 t ground ginger

½ t pepper

¼ t ground turmeric

4 skin-on salmon fillets (½ lb. each)

Preheat the oven to 450°F.

Tear the Swiss chard leaves off their stems in rough pieces. Put in a medium glass baking dish. SWOOPS the carrots and scatter over the greens.

In a small bowl, combine the brown sugar, cumin, paprika, smoked salt, ginger, pepper, and turmeric. Pour this rub mixture onto a plate in an even layer. SWOOPS the salmon fillets. Dip the flesh side of each fillet into the rub and shake off the excess. Place the fish skin side down on top of the chard and carrots in the baking dish. Roast in the oven for 8 minutes. (Do not overcook your fish or I will hunt you down and shame you—remember that it'll continue to cook after it's out of the oven.)

Floral-Rub Halibut with Spinach & Green Apples

PREP TIME: 10 MINUTES / TOTAL TIME: 20 MINUTES / SERVINGS: 4

....

1 (5-oz.) package baby spinach

SWOOPS

2 Granny Smith apples, cored and diced

1 T brown sugar

1 T ground sumac

1 T ground cardamom

1 t salt

1 t ground ginger

1 t nutmeg

½ t pepper

4 halibut fillets (½ lb. each)

¼ c chopped fresh mint

....

Preheat the oven to 450°F.

Place the spinach in a medium glass baking dish. SWOOPS the apples and scatter over the greens.

In a small bowl, combine the brown sugar, sumac, cardamom, salt, ginger, nutmeg, and pepper. Pour this rub mixture onto a plate in an even layer. SWOOPS the halibut fillets. Dip the flesh side of each fillet in the rub and shake off the excess. Place the fish skin side down on top of the spinach and apples in the baking dish. Roast in the oven for 10 minutes. (Do not overcook your fish or I will hunt you down and shame you—remember that it'll continue to cook after it's out of the oven.) Sprinkle the mint on top before serving.

WINE: *Rhône Blend*
PRODUCER: **Jean-Louis Chave Hermitage Blanc**
REGION: **Northern Rhône, France**

This halibut dish is anything but subtle. It calls for a big white wine. While some may turn to huge, over-oaked California Chardonnays, perhaps one should try a relatively unappreciated white Rhône. These usually tend to be full-bodied blends of Marsanne, Roussanne, Viognier, and Grenache Blanc. Among the white wines in this region, usually known for its reds, Chave Hermitage Blanc is at the head of the class. Hermitage is an extremely small, prestigious hilltop. The Chave family has been making wine since 1481 and arrived at Hermitage in the early 19th century. So they've had a little practice with making wine. This opulent wine is a blend of Roussanne and Marsanne, which pairs perfectly with this floral and buttery halibut.

OPP: **E. Guigal, Famille Perrin, M. Chapoutier**

BAND: **The New Mastersounds**
ALBUM: ***This Is What We Do***
YEAR/GENRE: **(2005), Jazz Funk**

The first time I heard The New Mastersounds, they were opening for Mofro for a Langerado night show. Beas, Sarah, Jody, and I needed to be practically carried out we were so blown away by their throwback groove jazz akin to Jimmy Smith but with a hefty dose of James Brown. They played my Gatsby birthday party: 200 people, black-tie, '20s style. It looked like a movie set. I tried to keep the band a surprise from my guests. The cocktail hour had a DJ in the side room. Then the band took the stage in the main room. My friend Allard noted on his way downstairs, "This DJ is great, he's playing lots of New Mastersounds!" "No, Allard, that IS The New Mastersounds." This dish is flowery like Daisy Buchanan.

WINE: **Gamay**
PRODUCER: **Domaine Jean Foillard 'Morgon - Cuvee Corcelette'**
REGION: **Beaujolais, France**

Most people associate Beaujolais with the light, relatively tasteless Nouveau wines that come out before Thanks-g. each year, but cru Beaujolais is another beast entirely. Of Beaujolais' 10 crus, Morgon is considered one of the best. This wine would definitely land on my Top 10 Wines in Life list. It's happiness with every sip and impresses a range of palates. Pure Gamay silk. This is a good example of an "opposites attract" pairing. The bright, silky, fruity Gamay is actually highlighted when pitted against herbs, crunchy kale, and acidic tomato. I discovered this wine at Marvin*, my favorite bistro in my 'hood (specifically, West Hollywood). If it's on any restaurant wine list, I order it for the table—its value is unparalleled.

*Other wines from Marvin; see page 173

OPP: **Domaine Lapierre, Guy Breton, Mee Godard, Olivier Merlin, Julie Balagny**

BAND: **Bruce Springsteen**
ALBUM: ***Born in the U.S.A.***
YEAR/GENRE: **(1984), Rock**

I didn't attend my first Bruce concerts until 2009 when I went with my friend Jelly. (His real name is Jim, but I have trouble calling any friends the same name as my dad.) We saw him at L.A. Memorial Coliseum and at Bonnaroo later that year. Almost ten years later, he's still blowing me away. *Springsteen on Broadway* was definitely the best show I've seen in the theater in years. It was a super special, intimate treat that I'll always feel fortunate to have experienced. This album, a commercial, heartland rock blockbuster, broke out The Boss worldwide. He's Bruce Summersteen for this dish. The herbal rub ties the grit to this main-dish music and will put you too on the map...in the kitchen.

Herbal-Rub Cod with Kale & Tomatoes

PREP TIME: 10 MINUTES / TOTAL TIME: 20 MINUTES / SERVINGS: 4

....

1 bunch kale

SWOOPS

2 large heirloom tomatoes, diced

1 T brown sugar

1 T fennel seed

1 T ground cardamom

1 t salt

1 t ground ginger

1 t allspice

½ t pepper

4 skin-on cod fillets (½ lb. each)

¼ c chopped fresh shiso

....

Preheat the oven to 450°F.

Tear the kale leaves off their stems in rough pieces. Put in a medium glass baking dish. SWOOPS. SWOOPS the tomatoes and scatter them over the greens.

In a small bowl, combine the brown sugar, fennel seed, cardamom, salt, ginger, allspice, and pepper. Pour this rub mixture onto a plate in an even layer. SWOOPS the cod fillets. Dip the flesh side of each fillet into the rub, and shake off the excess. Place the fish skin side down on top of the kale and tomatoes. Roast in the oven for 10 minutes. (Do not overcook your fish or I will hunt you down and shame you—remember that it'll continue to cook after it's out of the oven.) Sprinkle the shiso on top before serving.

Herbal-Rub Cod with
Kale & Tomatoes

Sweet-Rub Sea Bass with
Mixed Greens & Pomegranate

Sweet-Rub Sea Bass with Mixed Greens & Pomegranate

PREP TIME: 10 MINUTES / TOTAL TIME: 20 MINUTES / SERVINGS: 4

. . . .

1 bunch mixed greens (I like dandelion and beet greens), roughly chopped

SWOOPS

½ c pomegranate seeds

2 T brown sugar

1 T ground cinnamon

1 T ground cardamom

1 t salt

1 t ground ginger

1 t allspice

½ t pepper

¼ t ground turmeric

4 Chilean sea bass fillets (½ lb. each; make sure you're getting Patagonian Toothfish and not an imposter sea bass)

. . . .

Preheat the oven to 450°F.

Put the mixed greens in a medium glass baking dish. SWOOPS. Scatter the pomegranate seeds over the greens.

In a small bowl, combine the brown sugar, cinnamon, cardamom, salt, ginger, allspice, pepper, and turmeric. Pour this rub mixture onto a plate in an even layer. SWOOPS the sea bass fillets. Dip the flesh side of each fillet in the rub, and shake off the excess. Place the fish skin side down on top of the greens and pomegranate seeds. Roast in the oven for 10 minutes. (Do not overcook your fish or I will hunt you down and shame you—remember that it'll continue to cook after it's out of the oven.)

CHEF'S LAGNIAPPE LESSON: If you're in the Pacific Time Zone, make sure you get to the farmers' market when it opens at 9 a.m., so you're back home in time for 10 a.m. NFL kickoff.

WINE: *Melon de Bourgogne*
PRODUCER: **Domaine Pierre Luneau-Papin 'Excelsior'**
REGION: **Muscadet, Loire Valley, France**

This dry, light-bodied white from the western end of the Loire Valley, near Nantes, is made exclusively with Melon de Bourgogne grapes. These wines are lean-tasting with citrus or tart apple notes, and often have a salty aroma from the sea. Though most drink Muscadet when it is fresh and young, the best ones (like this) are actually longer-lived, since they undergo a process of "sur lie" aging, with extended lees and dead yeast cells contact. The Melon de Bourgogne grape benefits from this "sur lie" procedure because it adds weight and texture to an otherwise thin-tasting wine, rendering it pairable with the buttery, sweet sea bass and juicy, acidic pomegranate.

OPP: **Domaine de l'Ecu, Domaine de la Pépière, Domaine du Haut Bourg**

BAND: **Van Morrison**
ALBUM: *Moondance*
YEAR/GENRE: **(1970), Soul Rock**

This is another feel-good album and I'm confident you'll give me crazy love for this fish preparation by the time fall rolls in. I know it doesn't have the critical acclaim of *Astral Weeks* (which upon its release was a commercial flop), but these pairings are rooted in listenability. With its more composed songs and upbeat backing (particularly those signature horn blasts), there's no denying it. And look at the first half of the album: "And It Stoned Me," "Moondance," "Crazy Love," "Caravan," and "Into the Mystic." Besides maybe The Beatles or Stones, what other album from this period has that kind of Side-A song depth?

CHICKEN

Tastes like chicken? I guess this is meant to be a compliment, generally directed toward a seemingly adventurous alternative, aiming to temper the risk and render it safe. Which is generally why I find chicken boring. I do like it, I eat it, heck, sometimes I crave it. My natural affinity gravitates elsewhere. But since it's such a crowd-pleaser, I needed to be able to master it. Take a stab at these easy yet hopefully jazzed-up chicken recipes. I would suggest getting your chicken pre-cut if you're feeling queasy from having been in hard-core celebration mode or something. If not, you risk gagging when you hear the sound of the bones being cut or you see your mother reaching inside to remove the innards. (Did I mention that chicken's not my favorite?)

Chicken with Fennel, Blood Orange & Olives

PREP TIME: 30 MINUTES / TOTAL TIME: 1 HOUR 30 MINUTES / SERVINGS: 4

2 fennel bulbs, root ends trimmed, bulb cut into ¼-inch slices, and wispy green fronds reserved for garnish

1 large onion, chopped

2 blood oranges, 1 cut into ¼-inch pieces, 1 juiced

½ c green olives (Castelvetrano recommended), pitted and sliced

SWOOPS

1 whole chicken, quartered

2 t ground ginger

2 t garlic powder

¼ c chopped flat-leaf parsley

Preheat the oven to 400°F.

Combine the fennel, onion, blood orange pieces, and olives in a big-ass baking pan. SWOOPS and too-us!

Season the chicken pieces with the ginger and garlic powder, then SWOOPS. Place the chicken on top of everything in the pan and roast in the oven for 25 minutes.

Flip the chicken over and roast for another 25 minutes. Test to make sure it is fully cooked by pricking it with a fork. The juices that run out should be clear (not bloody). Sprinkle the parsley on top and serve!

WINE: **Sangiovese**
PRODUCER: **Poggio Antico 'Brunello di Montalcino'**
REGION: **Tuscany, Italy**
Big reds seem to own the winter like the Patriots do the Super Bowl. With herbal accents of fennel and savory accents of the god of olives, the Castelvetrano, I turn to a red that folds those layers in with big, winter-friendly fruit: Brunello di Montalcino. Made from the Brunello clone of the Sangiovese grape, these wines age for at least five years before release—that's a serious relationship in my book. But they are also some of the most food-friendly, with searing acidity that begs the complement of food. It rings particularly true for this Poggio Antico, which has some of the highest-elevation vineyards in Montalcino, an area in southern Tuscany.

OPP: **Altesino, Casanove di Neri, La Torre**

BAND: **Jimmy Smith**
ALBUM: *Back at the Chicken Shack*
YEAR/GENRE: **(1960), Jazz**
The Chicken Shack will be your go-to chicken dinner music. Oh, Jimmy, the things you do to me. He's just so smooth! With backing from Stanley Turrentine on sax and Kenny Burrell on guitar, this is one of those albums for any casual jazz fan who wants a few must-haves beyond *Kind of Blue*. I remember seeing Jimmy play when I first moved to L.A. at the famed Catalina Bar & Grill with my friends Phil and Amy, who were bent on seeing older musicians before they passed. Phil remembers me laughing during a break in between songs and Jimmy looking over and going, "What was that? A billy goat?!" When you have a laugh like mine, you tend to kind of tune those things out. So jazz up your winter chicken with Jimmy.

Chicken with Potatoes & Asparagus

PREP TIME: 30 MINUTES / TOTAL TIME: 1 HOUR 30 MINUTES / SERVINGS: 4

....

1 lb. Yukon Gold potatoes, cubed, skin-on

1 large onion, chopped

2 T peeled and chopped fresh ginger (about a 1-inch piece)

SWOOPS

1 whole chicken, quartered

2 t ground ginger

2 t garlic powder

1 bunch baby (needle) asparagus, cut into 2-inch pieces

¼ c chopped flat-leaf parsley

....

Preheat the oven to 400°F.

Combine the potatoes, onion, and chopped ginger in a big-ass baking pan. SWOOPS and too-us!

Season the chicken pieces with the ground ginger and garlic powder, then SWOOPS. Place the chicken on top of everything in the pan and roast in the oven for 25 minutes.

Flip the chicken over, add the asparagus, and roast for another 25 minutes. Test to make sure the chicken is fully cooked by pricking it with a fork. The juices that run out should be clear (not bloody). Sprinkle the parsley on top and serve!

Chicken with Potatoes
& Asparagus

Chicken with Cherries & Almonds

PREP TIME: 30 MINUTES / TOTAL TIME: 1 HOUR 30 MINUTES / SERVINGS: 4

....

2 c cherries, pitted and chopped

1 large sweet onion, chopped

1 T sugar

2 T peeled and chopped fresh ginger (about a 1-inch piece)

SWOOPS

1 whole chicken, quartered

2 t ginger powder

2 t garlic powder

¼ c chopped flat-leaf parsley

¼ c toasted chopped almonds

....

Preheat the oven to 400°F.

Place the cherries, sweet onion, sugar, and chopped ginger in a big-ass baking pan. SWOOPS and too-us!

Season the chicken pieces with the ginger and garlic powders, then SWOOPS. Place the chicken on top of everything in the pan and roast in the oven for 25 minutes.

Flip the chicken over and roast for another 25 minutes. Test to make sure it is fully cooked by pricking it with a fork. The juices that run out should be clear (not bloody).
Sprinkle the parsley and almonds on top and serve!

"And as he handed me a drink he began to hum a song
And all the boys there at the bar began to sign along
If you'll be my Dixie chicken, I'll be your Tennessee lamb
And we can walk together down in Dixieland"
— *Little Feat "Dixie Chicken"*

Chicken with Sweet
Potato & Squash

Chicken with Sweet Potato & Squash

PREP TIME: 30 MINUTES / TOTAL TIME: 1 HOUR 30 MINUTES / SERVINGS: 4

1 sweet potato, peeled, cut into ½-inch disks, then quartered

½ large butternut squash, peeled, seeded, and cut into 1-inch cubes (about 2 c)

2 medium onions, peeled and cut into 1-inch cubes

1 T fresh rosemary (2 little sprigs—great word)

1 T fresh thyme

2 T peeled and chopped fresh ginger (about a 1-inch piece)

SWOOPS

1 T brown sugar

1 t ground cinnamon

1 whole chicken, quartered

2 t ground ginger

2 t garlic powder

¼ c chopped flat-leaf parsley

Preheat the oven to 450°F.

Combine the sweet potato, butternut squash, onions, rosemary, thyme, and chopped ginger in a big-ass baking pan. SWOOPS and too-us! Sprinkle the brown sugar and cinnamon on top.

Season the chicken pieces with the ground ginger and garlic powder, then SWOOPS. Place the chicken on top of everything in the pan and roast in the oven for 25 minutes.

Flip the chicken over and roast for another 25 minutes. Test to make sure it is fully cooked by pricking it with a fork. The juices that run out should be clear (not bloody). Sprinkle the parsley on top and serve!

WINE: **Bordeaux Blend**
PRODUCER: **Lapostolle 'Clos Apalta'**
REGION: **Colchagua Valley, Chile**
Bordeaux blends are made almost all over the world, but this one is unique because its dominant grape is a less common variety: Carmenère. Carmenère is to Chile as Malbec is to Argentina—they both used to be just blending grapes in Bordeaux, but when grown in South America they have the ability to ripen fully and stand proudly and deliciously on their own. This is one of our favorites, and it is arguably the country's best. Rich autumn flavors of sweet potato and squash seasoned with sweet spices are met with the intensity and lift of this supreme blend. Anyone in the mood for more booze? (Jordan raises hand.) We can keep it in the family and douse a little Grand Marnier over the chicken. Heiress Alexandra Marnier Lapostolle founded Casa Lapostolle in 1994; her great-grandfather founded Grand Marnier.

OPP: **TerraNoble, Casa Silva, Montes**

BAND: **Natalie Cole**
ALBUM: *Unforgettable...with Love*
YEAR/GENRE: **(1991), Jazz**
Since the chickens are all Betti, I find it appropriate that she helps pick the album pairings, too. This was in high rotation in my former years and Jim particularly enjoys the final track where Natalie is dubbed with her dad Nat King Cole in harmony. At the time it was a big deal—a real sonic marvel—and thankfully it hasn't aged into something that sounds gimmicky. It also exposed and ultimately gave me an appreciation for some of the Great American Songbook that I would have otherwise let fade into the background over the din of life and my inherently loud voice.

WINTER: Mushroom Gremolata Sauce

SPRING: Artichoke Gremolata Sauce

STEAK

No matter the season, the Zuckers think a perfect steak is just simply doused in salt and pepper and grilled on the fireplace (key technique) until medium rare. The only element we'd take a seasonal journey on is the accompanying sauce. Gremolata is traditionally an herbed condiment made with citrus zest, parsley, and garlic. In these recipes, I used its essence as inspiration for four scrumptious steak sauces. Top it, dip it, take your seasonal trip in it. Since you might not have a kitchen fireplace with a grill rack installed (props to my folks for the pimped-out design element), I use a grill pan in these recipes. The steak won't come out as perfectly smoke-infused, but this is how I do it too when I'm not in our properly equipped Vermont home.

SUMMER: Smoky Poblano Gremolata Sauce

FALL: Red Wine–Shallot Gremolata Sauce

WINE: **Malbec**
PRODUCER: **Catena**
REGION: **Mendoza, Argentina**

The one country that will give the U.S. competition as the world's biggest steak lover is Argentina. The go-to wine there for accompanying steak is Malbec, with its bold flavors and soft tannins that will match particularly well with savory mushrooms. The Mendoza region of Argentina is the country's largest and most well-known, and family-owned Bodega Catena Zapata was instrumental in building the area's reputation for high-quality Malbec. Catena blends Malbec vineyards from various elevations ranging from the high Uco Valley down to the Mendoza floor to successfully reap all the benefits that Malbec has to offer. The higher altitude vines add freshness and acidity, and the valley floor vines offer intensity and structure. Catena is a pioneer in extreme high-altitude vinification.

OPP: **Andeluna, Poesia, Chakana 'Cueva de las Manos,' Bodega Cicchitti**

BAND: **The Black Keys**
ALBUM: *Rubber Factory*
YEAR/GENRE: **(2004), Rock**
Now we are hitting the meaty albums. This is pure, gritty, in-your-face, blues-fueled rock and roll. The third album from the Ohio duo put them on the nationwide "cool kids" radar, and within a few years they started recording with Danger Mouse and playing arenas. Recorded in an abandoned tire factory, the warm distorted fuzz of "10 A.M. Automatic" and "Girl Is on My Mind" are as undeniable as a perfectly cooked steak with a Malbec. I finally got to see these guys in 2010 at Central Park Summerstage in New York and they cooked up a smoking show.

Steak with Mushroom Gremolata Sauce

PREP TIME: 15 MINUTES / TOTAL TIME: 30 MINUTES / SERVINGS: 4

½ c plus 1 T olive oil

2 c cremini mushrooms, sliced

2 t chopped garlic (about 2 small cloves)

½ t salt

¼ t pepper

1 lime, juiced and zested (about 2 T juice and 1 T zest)

½ c roughly chopped fresh parsley

2 T heavy cream

SWOOPS

4 steaks (½ lb. each; suggested cut: rib-eye)

Heat 1 T of the olive oil in a pan on medium-high heat. Add the mushrooms and garlic and sauté, giving the occasional stir, until the mushrooms are cooked through, about 5 minutes. Add the salt, pepper, and lime juice. Sauté for another 2 minutes.

Add the mushroom mixture to a blender along with the lime zest, parsley, cream, and the remaining ½ cup olive oil. Blend until smooth, unless you like it chunky, in which case, blend until chunky. (Mad Libs break: I like my steak sauce like I like my _____.)
noun

Heat a grill to medium-high. SWOOPS the steaks, then grill to medium-rare, about 4 minutes per side, depending on the thickness of the meat. Remove from the grill and transfer to a cutting board. Let the steaks rest for 5 minutes before serving.

Transfer the steaks to plates and smother with the mushroom gremolata sauce. OMG, I know. The gremolata is so good. You're going to want to eat it with a spoon, or smear it on top of toasted bread for a variation on bruschetta.

Steak with Artichoke Gremolata Sauce

PREP TIME: 15 MINUTES / TOTAL TIME: 30 MINUTES / SERVINGS: 4

1 can artichoke hearts (about 6), drained and quartered

½ c roughly chopped fresh parsley

¼ c olive oil

2 T heavy cream

½ lime, juiced and zested (about 1 T juice and ½ T zest)

2 garlic cloves, roughly chopped (about 1 T)

½ t salt

¼ t pepper

SWOOPS

4 steaks (½ lb. each; suggested cut: rib-eye)

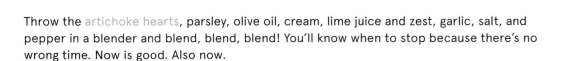

Throw the artichoke hearts, parsley, olive oil, cream, lime juice and zest, garlic, salt, and pepper in a blender and blend, blend, blend! You'll know when to stop because there's no wrong time. Now is good. Also now.

Heat a grill to medium-high. SWOOPS the steaks, then grill to medium-rare, about 4 minutes per side, depending on the thickness of the meat. Remove from the grill and transfer to a cutting board. Let the steaks rest for 5 minutes before serving.

Transfer the steaks to plates and smother with the artichoke gremolata sauce. Hear the angels sing.

WINE: **Cabernet Franc**
PRODUCER: **Olga Raffault 'Chinon Les Picasses'**
REGION: **Chinon, Loire Valley, France**
Artichoke can be pesky and tricky to pair with, clashing with many wines. So instead of turning to a tasteless fraternity beer or bland white, we're leaning on a Cab Franc with classic herbaceous notes and bright acidity. Uber-traditional versions from Chinon, in the heart of the Loire Valley, showcase the grape at its best, all dewy grass and turned earth and crunchy fruit. You can't really get more traditional than Olga Raffault, who ran this benchmark winery for more than fifty years. The trend of badass ladies at the helm continues—her granddaughter Sylvie now runs the estate.

OPP: **Bernard Baudry, Catherine et Pierre Breton, Jacky Blot, Domaine Laporte**

BAND: **Stevie Wonder**
ALBUM: *Original Musiquarium*
YEAR/GENRE: **(1982), R&B**
"Boogie on Reggae Woman" OG. This album is a collection of singles and hits from the previous ten years and they're all the main course. One of the new tunes on here is the original version of the punchy groover "Do I Do" which clocks in at more than 10 minutes and features Dizzy Gillespie blowing trumpet and Stevie's eventual bandleader Nathan Watts laying down a filthy bassline. When Stevie's set was rained out at JazzFest in 2015, my crew sheltered in the grandstands and ate cochon de lait po' boys. Once we acquiesced to the rain gods, we embraced the rain and everyone ran out into the mud for a makeout social. Kissing in the rain is as joyous as Stevie and steak. I can't imagine any human being able to instantly put folks in a good mood quite like Stevie, a legendary "main course" of music.

Steak with All Four Sauces

WINE: **GSM**
PRODUCER: **Torbreck 'Juveniles'**
REGION: **Barossa Valley, Australia**

GSM is short for a Grenache/Syrah/Mourvèdre blend, a classic from the Côtes du Rhône that has been adopted around the world. Torbreck is another one of our favorite Australian winemakers. An unoaked marvel! This wine's lack of oak tannin along with the low tannin structure of the dominant Grenache grape pairs well with the spicy and smoky aspects of the poblano pepper in this steak sauce. Please send written personal thank yous for this pairing, gushing about how right I am. Feed the beast!

OPP: **Clarendon Hills, Dandelion, Shinas Estates**

BAND: **Beastie Boys**
ALBUM: *Paul's Boutique*
YEAR/GENRE: **(1989), Hip-Hop, Rock**

Meaty. Smoky. Spicy. My bandwidth for hip-hop in general is limited, but I've always loved me some Beastie Boys. They've set a very high bar for any other aspiring Jewish rappers out there. After their audacious debut, *Licensed To III*, they followed it up with a more mature offering that folds in layers and layers of samples, turns the groove up a few notches (versus the pure frat rap sing-alongs), and boldly telegraphs where they were stylistically headed. It's fun and juvenile in just the right ways, which is why I'm pairing it with a wine that will hopefully make you feel the same.

Steak with Smoky Poblano Gremolata Sauce

PREP TIME: 30 MINUTES / TOTAL TIME: 45 MINUTES / SERVINGS: 4

....

SWOOPS

2 large poblano peppers

½ c roughly chopped fresh parsley

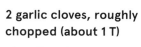

2 garlic cloves, roughly chopped (about 1 T)

¼ c olive oil

1 lime, juiced and zested (about 2 T juice and 1 T zest)

2 T heavy cream

½ t salt

¼ t pepper

4 steaks (½ lb. each; suggested cut: rib-eye)

....

Heat a grill to medium-high. SWOOPS the poblano peppers and cook on the grill, flipping, until they are charred and soft, about 10 minutes per side. Transfer to a cutting board, and let cool. Remove the skins and seeds (running the peppers under cold water helps with this), and give them a rough chop. Add them to a blender along with the parsley, garlic, olive oil, lime juice and zest, cream, salt, and pepper. Blend until smooth, just like the ocean under the moon. (Rob Thomas and Santana's ocean is apparently more like a lake.)

SWOOPS the steaks, then cook on the grill until medium-rare, about 4 minutes per side, depending on the thickness of the meat. Remove from the grill and transfer to a cutting board. Let the steaks rest for 5 minutes before serving.

Transfer the steaks to plates and smother with the poblano gremolata sauce. Nom, nom, nom.

Steak with Red Wine-Shallot Gremolata Sauce

PREP TIME: 15 MINUTES / TOTAL TIME: 30 MINUTES / SERVINGS: 4

¼ c olive oil

1 large shallot, chopped

1 medium yellow onion, chopped

3 garlic cloves, chopped (about 1½ T)

1 c red wine (something you'd drink)

½ c roughly chopped fresh parsley

2 T heavy cream

½ lime, juiced and zested (about 1 T juice and ½ T zest)

½ t salt

¼ t pepper

SWOOPS

4 steaks (½ lb. each; suggested cut: rib-eye)

Heat the olive oil in a skillet over medium-high heat. Add the shallot, onion, and garlic and sauté until translucent and slightly browned, 2 to 3 minutes. Add the red wine, bring to a boil, and cook until the liquid is reduced by half, about 5 minutes. Turn off heat and give it a stir.

Throw the shallot mixture in a blender along with the parsley, remaining ¼ cup olive oil, the cream, lime juice and zest, salt, and pepper. Blend until smooth, Smooth Operator status. (Does it bother you when song lyrics say things like "coast to coast, L.A. to Chicago" even though Chicago's not coastal?)

Heat a grill to medium-high. SWOOPS the steaks, then grill to medium-rare, about 4 minutes per side, depending on the thickness of the meat. Remove from the grill and transfer to a cutting board. Let the steaks rest for 5 minutes before serving.

Transfer the steaks to plates and smother with the red wine–shallot gremolata sauce. Decline the ensuing marriage proposals.

WINE: **Cabernet Sauvignon**
PRODUCER: **Shafer 'One Point Five'**
REGION: **Napa Valley, California**

This is my drafting wine with my friend Andee. Fantasy Football draft is our favorite night of the year. Not all leagues can manage live drafts, so for the ones conducted online, we'll sit together with our laptops, load the draft apps, drink our One Point Five, and squeal over our Jimmy Graham steal. A big steak and a big Cab yields a big win. 100% new French Oak for 20 months makes this a big strapping man of a wine! Most Napa family-owned wineries are on their second generation of ownership. However, the father-and-son Shafer team have been figuring things out together, blurring the two-generation timeline into a one point five generation owned winery. To the Shafer Winery, "One Point Five" wine equates to family. To me and Andee, it's touchdown city.

OPP: **Plumpjack, Heitz, Cade**

BAND: **Led Zeppelin**
ALBUM: *Houses of the Holy*
YEAR/GENRE: **(1973), Blues Rock**

While so much of Zep's catalog could pair with a big steak dinner, I ultimately chose *Houses of the Holy*. Maybe because my high school gymnastics routine was to "Song Remains the Same," maybe because I'm obsessed with the Giant's Causeway in Northern Ireland (on the album cover), or maybe it's just because it's got some of my enduring favorites like "No Quarter," "Over the Hills and Far Away," and "Rain Song" with its verbose rock strings. It's the first album to get a name title instead of a number (though neither the band name or title appear on the outside sleeve as with previous records); we're pairing the One Point Five with what would have been Zeppelin Five.

MEATBALLS

Tee hee hee. Everything's better in a ball! Seriously: They have no bones, it's somewhat socially acceptable to eat them with your hands, and they're adorbs. They're also a great main dish with a pass-around vibe, which is my fave part of any party or smorgasbord.

Ahi Tuna Balls with Wasabi-Avocado Dip

PREP TIME: 15 MINUTES / TOTAL TIME: 45 MINUTES / SERVINGS: 6

....

MEATBALLS:

1 lb. ahi tuna, ground or finely chopped

1 lemon, juiced and zested

1 lime, juiced and zested

1 orange, juiced and zested

¼ c finely chopped scallions

1 T finely chopped peeled fresh ginger

1 T panko breadcrumbs

1 T black sesame seeds

1 T toasted sesame oil

1 t chili sesame oil

1 t chili paste

Salt and pepper

1 T olive oil

DIP:

½ c mayonnaise

½ c full-fat plain Greek yogurt

1 T wasabi paste

½ lime, juiced

1 t garlic (about 1 small clove)

1 avocado, halved and pitted

Salt and pepper

....

TO MAKE THE MEATBALLS: Combine the tuna, citrus juice and zest, scallions, ginger, panko, sesame seeds, toasted sesame oil, chili sesame oil, and chili paste. Season with salt and pepper, then mix well using your clean, bare hands (rings removed).

Heat the olive oil in a skillet over medium-high heat. Scoop out small handfuls of the tuna mixture and form into mini burger patty shapes or balls, about 2-inch diameter. Cook the patties/balls in the oil for a minute on each side (work in batches if necessary). They should not be fully cooked through—you're going for more of a sear to mimic a tartare. (Do you enjoy saying "tuna tartare tartine" as much as I do?) Transfer the patties/balls to a paper towel–lined plate to drain and cool. Put your rings back on.

TO MAKE THE DIP: In a blender, combine the mayonnaise and yogurt until smooth. Add the wasabi paste, lime juice, and garlic. Blend until smooth. Scoop the meat of the avocado into the blender and continue blending until smooth, scraping down the sides in between pulses to incorporate everything. Season with salt and pepper. Transfer to a bowl and serve with the meatballs for dipping.

CHEF'S LAGNIAPPE LESSON: For those of you still working to lose those damn 10 pounds you mysteriously gained one year or over a few years (who knew the "10" in 2010 was going to be so prophetic?), I understand that you're hoping to limit your carbs. Just dip and eat your tuna balls. For the rest of you, go ahead and shmear some of the wasabi cream onto a mini dinner roll and sandwich a tuna patty in there to make a slider.

WINE: *Zinfandel Blend*
PRODUCER: **The Prisoner**
REGION: **Napa Valley, California**
Although no longer made by Orin Swift, this is my go-to wine if I'm in an area that doesn't source bottles from smaller local wineries. The Prisoner is reliable and has wide enough distribution that it'll be an oasis in a desert of "grocery store" wines where I'm scrambling to find something I can swallow. This red blend is special because the Zinfandel is blended with Cabernet Sauvignon as well as the more (other) likely suspects of Petite Sirah, Syrah, and Charbono. Charbono, also an "endangered species" akin to the Bonarda of Argentina, save them all! This wine is a crowd-pleaser and will be enjoyed while preparing a meal, during a meal, and after a meal—it is an equal-opportunity guzzler.

OPP: **Orin Swift '8 Years in the Desert,' Gamble Family Vineyards, Day**

BAND: **James Brown**
ALBUM: *Ain't It Funky*
YEAR/GENRE: **(1970), R&B, Funk, Soul**
This Prisoner wine is paired with a man who's done time and also been a "Prisoner of Love." Ladies and gentlemen, boys and girls, will you welcome please, the Godfather of Soul, Mr. James Brown! You can't really go wrong with any album up through the mid-'70s thanks to a backing band that included Maceo Parker, Fred Wesley, Clyde Stubblefield, and Bernard Odum, among many others. This album, his 31st (!), is an energetic romp through jazz, R&B, and New Orleans funk though it features next to no singing from the man himself—just killer jams. A proper winter pick-me-up, you'll be warding off the cold weather lull in no time and having a ball, a tuna ball!

WINE: Rosé
PRODUCER: Kunin 'Phoebe'
REGION: Santa Barbara, California
We stampeded the Kunin tasting room in Santa Barbara's Funk Zone to see what the late Seth Kunin's legacy would pour us, and this was the standout. The Funk Zone is Santa Barbara's hipster warehouse district that bred tasting rooms, art galleries, microbreweries, farm-to-table restaurants, and more. Kunin is a natural winery and a pioneer California Rhône Ranger. This rosé is Grenache based, a fun, bright pairing with this Greek-inspired tzatziki/yogurt dip.

OPP: Red Car, Peay, Matthiasson

BAND: The Derek Trucks Band
ALBUM: *Songlines*
YEAR/GENRE: (2006), Blues Rock
Derek Trucks' lineage is part of rock royalty: His uncle is founding Allman Brothers Band drummer Butch Trucks. A recognized guitar prodigy, Derek formed DTB at age 15 and by 20 he was an official member of the ABB. He married fellow kickass musician Susan Tedeschi and the two toured as Soul Stew Revival before officially launching their own band in 2010. I caught them in 2006 at the John Anson Ford and it was the concert of the year. I had also developed a full girl crush on Susan. She was wearing what my friend Sarah and I called a purple Peter Pan dress with a tiered leaved skirt, and hefty four-inch heels. She owned it up there. I take my dad every year to see one of their shows during their Beacon Theater residency.

Lamb Meatballs with Cucumber-Mint Dip

PREP TIME: 25 MINUTES / TOTAL TIME: 1 HOUR / SERVINGS: 6

MEATBALLS:

1 lb. ground lamb

3 garlic cloves, chopped (about 1½ T)

¼ c chopped fresh rosemary

1 egg

1 T breadcrumbs

Salt and pepper

Olive oil, for coating

DIP:

1 c full-fat plain Greek yogurt

½ c chopped fresh mint

½ c chopped cucumber

1 T lemon juice

1 t cayenne pepper

Salt and pepper

TO MAKE THE MEATBALLS: Preheat the oven to 400°F.

Combine the ground lamb, garlic, rosemary, egg, and breadcrumbs in a bowl. Season with salt and pepper, then mix well using your clean, bare hands (rings removed). Form the mixture into little meatballs, about 2-inch diameter, and place on a foil-lined baking sheet. Wash your hands and put your rings back on. Coat with olive oil. Bake the lamb meatballs in the oven for about 12 minutes, until cooked through. Remove from the oven and transfer to a paper towel–lined plate to drain.

TO MAKE THE DIP: Throw the yogurt, mint, cucumber, lemon juice, and cayenne into a blender and blend, blend, blend until smooth. Season with salt and pepper. Transfer to a bowl and serve with the meatballs for dipping.

WINTER   SPRING   SUMMER   FALL

Lamb Meatballs with Yogurt Dip

Chicken Hot Wing Meatballs with Cool Blue Cheese Dip

PREP TIME: 15 MINUTES / TOTAL TIME: 1 HOUR / SERVINGS: 6

WINE: Sparkling
PRODUCER: Podere il Saliceto 'Bi Fri'
REGION: Emilia-Romagna, Italy

This wine, made with Trebbiano Modenese and Sauvignon Blanc grapes in the Emilia-Romagna region of Italy, borders on a beer vibe. Pair it up with the "wings" element of the dish to emulate an upscale version of your local, divey sports bar from the comfort of your home. This wine is refermented in the bottle under a crown cap like a beer bottle, creating large, soft bubbles minimizing its acidity and preventing it from being austere. Podere il Saliceto focuses mainly on sparkling wine, predominantly Lambruscos...and now this fun, effervescent project.

OPP: **Ca' dei Zago, La Staffa, Bisson**

BAND: Bob Marley
ALBUM: *Kaya*
YEAR/GENRE: (1978), Reggae

Big surprise, I know, I picked a Bob Marley album for a summer dish. I'm not reinventing the wheel here. Thing is, Bob is undeniable. His mellifluous melodies, chill vibes, and proverb-like lyricism make him the legend he is. I, too, had a Bob poster in my college dorm room, "Stir It Up" is one of a select few songs I learned to play on the bass, and he was my father's favorite topic of conversation with my Grandma Gracie's Jamaican caretaker. Coming off the previous year's fiery *Exodus*, *Kaya* is all peace, love, and ganja with "Sun Is Shining," Satisfy My Soul," and "Easy Skanking." Wash it all down with some Bi Fri as Bob sings about being free.

MEATBALLS:

1 lb. ground chicken

¼ c hot wing sauce (if you can't find some, mix together 2 T hot sauce and 2 T melted butter)

1 T finely chopped garlic (about 2 cloves)

1 T flour

3 scallions, finely chopped

Salt and pepper

Olive oil, for coating

DIP:

1 c finely chopped Cabrales blue cheese

½ c full-fat plain Greek yogurt

1 T heavy cream

1 T fresh lemon juice

1 T chopped chives

Salt and pepper

TO MAKE THE MEATBALLS: Preheat the oven to 400°F.

Combine the chicken, hot wing sauce, garlic, flour, and scallions in a bowl. Season with salt and pepper, then mix thoroughly with clean, bare hands (rings removed). There's really no substitute for using your hands here. I encourage getting dirty in the kitchen. Form the mixture into little meatballs, about 2-inch diameter, and place on a foil-lined baking sheet. Wash your hands and put your rings back on. Coat with some olive oil. Bake the chicken meatballs in the oven for about 12 minutes, until cooked through. Remove from the oven and transfer to a paper towel–lined plate to drain.

TO MAKE THE DIP: Throw the blue cheese, yogurt, cream, lemon juice, and chives into a blender and blend, blend, blend until smooth. Season with salt and pepper. Transfer to a bowl and serve with the meatballs for dipping.

Chicken Hot Wing Meatballs
with Cool Blue Cheese Dip

WINE: **Mourvèdre**
PRODUCER: **Domaine Tempier**
REGION: **Bandol, France**
When I think of autumn, I think of football, a rugged sport. Bandol is an equally rugged red wine. From Provence in the south of France, it can be tannic when young. Like its rosé Bandol, Domaine Tempier's red Bandol is clearly the top of the class, made mostly with Mourvèdre. Keeping to tradition, Domaine Tempier ages their wine for the mandatory 18 months in oak, resulting in a big, burly wine. The dark olive tones and aroma of the Bandol work very well with the gamey duck and mustard in the marmalade. We're matching strong, brute forces from all directions with this one.

OPP: **Château de Pibarnon, La Bastide Blanche, Château Pradeaux, Bastide de la Ciselette**

BAND: **Cannonball Adderley**
ALBUM: *Somethin' Else*
YEAR/GENRE: **(1958), Jazz, Hard Bop**
Start out with some "Autumn Leaves." Also, more balls, cannon ones. Don't pull a party fowl and serve duck with bad music. For being such a relatively big man, Cannonball played a relatively small instrument (an alto sax, specifically). Once known as "cannibal" because of his big appetite, Adderley quickly became a figurehead in the jazz community to the extent that Miles Davis contributed to this album—which also included drummer Art Blakey and pianist Hank Jones—before inviting the saxophonist to contribute to *Milestones* and *Kind of Blue*. An all-star band for the *Band*ol wine.

Duck Meatballs with Onion Marmalade Dip

PREP TIME: 1 HOUR 30 MINUTES   /   TOTAL TIME: 2 HOURS 30 MINUTES   /   SERVINGS: 8

MEATBALLS:

2 duck breasts

1 T olive oil, plus more for coating

1 medium yellow onion, chopped

1 leek, white and light green parts only, thinly sliced **(see 🐷 page 37)**

4 garlic cloves, chopped (about 2 T)

½ lb. shiitake mushrooms

1 plum, pitted and roughly chopped

Salt and pepper

½ c chopped fresh parsley

2 T panko breadcrumbs

2 T tomato paste

2 T grated Parmesan cheese

DIP:

3 T butter

1 large sweet onion, chopped

1 small yellow onion, chopped

1 T light brown sugar

½ c dried cranberries

½ c water

1 t whole-grain mustard

2 T red wine

Salt and pepper

1 c full-fat plain Greek yogurt

TO MAKE THE MEATBALLS: Preheat the oven to 400°F.

Remove the fatty top layer of the duck breasts, chop, and set aside. Cut the breast meat into 1-inch cubes and freeze for an hour (my mother and I put them on a covered cookie sheet).

Heat the 1 tablespoon of olive oil in a skillet over medium heat. Add the onion and sauté for a minute. Add the leek and stir. Add the garlic, shiitakes, and plum. Stir. Season with salt and pepper.

Throw the duck breast meat and pan contents into a food processor. Blend until smooth. Add the parsley, panko, tomato paste, Parmesan, and 1 teaspoon of the reserved chopped duck fat to the mixture. Continue blending until smooth.

Scoop the duck mixture into little balls, about 2-inch diameter, and place on a foil-lined baking sheet. Coat with some olive oil. Bake the duck meatballs in the oven for about 15 minutes, until cooked through and starting to brown. Remove from the oven and transfer to a paper towel-lined plate to drain.

TO MAKE THE DIP: Heat the butter in a skillet over medium heat. Add all of the onions and sauté, with the occasional stir, until softening and starting to brown, about 8 minutes. Stir in the brown sugar, cranberries, water, and mustard. Cook, stirring constantly, until almost all of the liquid is absorbed, about 10 minutes. Add the red wine and season with salt and pepper. Stir. Lower the heat and simmer until thickened, about 10 more minutes. Transfer to a blender, add the yogurt, and blend, blend, blend until smooth. Transfer to a bowl and serve with the meatballs for dipping.

WINTER   SPRING   SUMMER   FALL

PASTA

When I was a kid, I would dream about jumping into the *Strega Nona* book (by Tomie dePaola) and eating my way out of the noodle world. I may have that dream again tonight. These pastas are hopefully a departure from the standard marinara sauce, celebrating each season's bounties along the way.

Sausage, Mustard & Spinach Pasta

PREP TIME: 10 MINUTES / TOTAL TIME: 30 MINUTES / SERVINGS: 6

1 (1-lb.) box pasta (your favorite shape; I like orecchiette)

SWOOPS

¼ c olive oil

1 large shallot, minced

½ medium onion, finely chopped

½ t salt

¼ t pepper

4 Italian sausage links, casings removed, halved lengthwise and chopped

1 (5-oz.) package spinach (about 3 c)

2 T whole-grain mustard

½ c chopped fresh flat-leaf parsley

2 garlic cloves, minced (about 1 T)

1 c grated Parmesan cheese

Bring a pot of salted water to a boil and add the pasta. Cook according to the instructions on the box. Drain, reserving 2 tablespoons of the cooking water. Transfer the pasta to a bowl and SWOOPS. (You can have the pasta cooking while you make the sauce—that way it's easy to add in a bit of the starchy pasta water.)

Heat the olive oil in a skillet over medium-high heat and add the shallot and onion. Sauté for 3 minutes, until slightly translucent. Season with the salt and pepper and give it a stir. Add the sausage and spinach and cook until the sausage is fully cooked through, about 7 minutes. Add the mustard and parsley and cook for 2 more minutes. Add the garlic and reserved pasta water and cook for another minute, stirring occasionally. Pour everything over the pasta. Add the Parmesan and toss, too-us, 2-us that soo-wus-idge (sausage).

Sausage, Mustard
& Spinach Pasta

Morel Pasta

PREP TIME: 10 MINUTES / TOTAL TIME: 30 MINUTES / SERVINGS: 6

1 (1-lb.) box pasta (your favorite shape; I like fusilli)

SWOOPS

¼ c olive oil

5 medium shallots, minced

½ t salt

¼ t pepper

½ lb. morel mushrooms, roughly chopped

4 T (½ stick) unsalted butter

1 c lovage, chopped

2 lemons, zested (about ¼ c)

4 garlic cloves, minced (about 2 T)

1 c grated Parmesan cheese

Bring a pot of salted water to a boil and add the pasta. Cook according to the instructions on the box. Drain, reserving 2 tablespoons of the cooking water. Transfer the pasta to a bowl and SWOOPS. (You can have the pasta cooking while you make the sauce—that way it's easy to add in a bit of the starchy pasta water.)

Heat the olive oil in a skillet over medium-high heat and add the shallots. Sauté for 3 minutes, until slightly translucent. Season with the salt and pepper and give it a stir. Add the morels and cook for another 2 minutes. Add the butter and stir through. Add the lovage, lemon zest, and garlic. Add the reserved pasta water and cook for another 2 minutes, stirring occasionally. Pour everything over the pasta. Add the Parmesan and toss, too-us, 2-us that oo-wus-im soo-wus. (awesome sauce).

WINE: **Vinho Verde**
PRODUCER: **Caves de Cerca 'Famega'**
REGION: **Minho, Portugal**
This Vinho Verde is made with the Arinto, Loureiro, and Trajadura grapes in Portugal and literally translates to "green wine," but "green" designates "young" in this case. Though not quite considered a semi-sparkling wine, it usually has some effervescence. This wine dances on the palate due to a natural secondary fermentation that happens in bottle. Many Vinho Verde producers in the market cheat and inject carbon dioxide to obtain that quintessential delicate effervescence, but not this one! Its pétillance makes it a party in a bottle, perfect for celebrating this confetti dish.

OPP: **Soalheiro, Anselmo Mendes, Casa do Valle**

BAND: **Jamiroquai**
ALBUM: *Emergency on Planet Earth*
YEAR/GENRE: **(1993), NuFunk**
The debut album from the electronic-laced space cowboy Jay Kay, Jamiroquai's music has retained its strength and integrity two decades on. It was certainly a soundtrack to more than a few dance parties in college that I feel like made liberal use of confetti. Or maybe that's just what they sound like. The thing is I still like dancing to it and now I do grownup things like cook to it and entertain with it as pre-game cocktail or post-dinner pick-me-up. While it's not quite virtual insanity, which would come three albums later, it was the template for a sophisticated dance party, to be sure.

Summer Squash Confetti Pasta

PREP TIME: 10 MINUTES / TOTAL TIME: 30 MINUTES / SERVINGS: 6

1 (1-lb.) box pasta (your favorite shape; I like linguine)

SWOOPS

½ c olive oil

1 medium onion, finely chopped (about 1 c)

Salt and pepper

1½ c baby tomatoes, halved and lightly salted (I like to use red and orange for the rainbow confetti effect)

2 small summer squash, grated (about 2 cups)

2 small zucchini, grated (about 2 cups)

2 garlic cloves, minced (about 1 T)

½ c chopped fresh chives

½ c chopped fresh mint

½ c chopped fresh tarragon

1 c grated Parmesan cheese

Bring a pot of salted water to a boil and add the pasta. Cook according to the instructions on the box. Drain, reserving 2 tablespoons of the cooking water. Transfer the pasta to a bowl and SWOOPS. (You can have the pasta cooking while you make the sauce—that way it's easy to add in a bit of the starchy pasta water.)

Heat ¼ cup of the olive oil in a skillet over medium-high heat and add the onion. Sauté for 3 minutes, until slightly translucent. Season with the salt and pepper and give it a stir. Add the tomatoes and cook for another 3 minutes, stirring occasionally. Once the tomatoes have started to cook down and ooze, add the remaining ¼ cup of olive oil. Stir. Add the grated squash and zucchini, 1 cup at a time, seasoning with salt and pepper each time, and cook, stirring, for about 2 minutes, until everything is well incorporated. Add the garlic and reserved pasta water and cook for another 2 minutes, stirring occasionally. Turn off the heat and stir in the chives, mint, and tarragon. Pour everything over the pasta. Add the Parmesan and toss, too-us, 2-us that summuh squash (summer squash).

Summer Squash
Confetti Pasta

"They say you gotta stay hungry
Hey baby I'm just about starving tonight
I'm dying for some action
I'm sick of sitting 'round here trying to write this book
I need a love reaction
Come on now baby gimme just one look"
— *Bruce Springsteen "Dancing in the Dark"*

Uni Eggplant Pasta

PREP TIME: 10 MINUTES / TOTAL TIME: 30 MINUTES / SERVINGS: 6

1 (1-lb.) box pasta
(your favorite shape;
I like rigatoni)

SWOOPS

¼ c olive oil

5 medium shallots, minced

½ t salt

¼ t pepper

1 large eggplant, cubed

4 T (½ stick) unsalted butter

1 c (about 8 oz.) uni
(sea urchin roe)

1 c chopped fresh
flat-leaf parsley

2 lemons, zested (about ¼ c)

4 garlic cloves, minced
(about 2 T)

1 T red pepper flakes

1 c grated Parmesan cheese

Bring a pot of salted water to a boil and add the pasta. Cook according to the instructions on the box. Drain, reserving 2 tablespoons of the cooking water. Transfer the pasta to a bowl and SWOOPS. (You can have the pasta cooking while you make the sauce—that way it's easy to add in a bit of the starchy pasta water.)

Heat the olive oil in a skillet over medium-high heat and add the shallots. Sauté for 3 minutes, until slightly translucent. Season with the salt and pepper and give it a stir. Add the eggplant. Add the butter and stir through. Cook for another 5 minutes. Meanwhile, puree the uni lobes in a mini food processor until smooth and add to the eggplant sauce. Add the parsley, lemon zest, garlic, and red pepper flakes. Add the reserved pasta water and cook, stirring, for another 2 minutes. Pour everything over the pasta. Add the Parmesan and toss, too-us, 2-us! It's like buttah (butter)!

WINE: **Negrette**
PRODUCER: **Château Flotis**
REGION: **Fronton, France**
Negrette is a pretty rare red grape that originates in Fronton, a small appellation in southwest France. It's an earthy beast! This wine showcases dense earth, crushed flowers, fresh mud, and smoked meats. It's a rustic wine for rustic wine drinkers! Not for the faint of heart. Matt* Kaner poured me this wine at his restaurant Good Measure and sent me on my merry way. This is an umami trifecta bomb—uni + eggplant + Negrette! The gaminess of a Negrette parties with the visceral uni and gets touched inappropriately yet is well received in the mosh pit of eggplant sauce.

*Other wines from Matt: see pages 138, 147, 163, 164 & 168

OPP: **Château Bellevue la Forêt, Château Bouissel, Château Coutinel**

BAND: **Khurangbin**
ALBUM: *The Universe Smiles Upon You*
YEAR/GENRE: **(2015), Psychedelic Rock**
Groove to *The UNIverse Smiles Upon You* while you slurp your uni! This one I discovered eating at MTN on Abbot Kinney in Venice with two of my besties. The "People Everywhere" track had me grooving on my barstool. I went to Shazam it but Beansie made the call before my phone could. That's my Beansie. Though this trio formed in Texas, the band name is the Thai word for airplane (technically, "engine fly"). And while it might sound like you have a mouthful of marbles trying to say the name, the band's sound is as smooth and silky as those pajama pants you bought on your last Southeast Asia vacation.

QUINOA

Welcome to my quinoa world tour! The gluten-free should get as much love as the vegetarians! As a self-proclaimed carboholic, I'll take my carbs in any form. You don't need to be battling celiac to love quinoa. It's so versatile and functional, it can wear many hats on a menu. From salad to side, it's a category-hopper. Spruce it up with all of the other showstopper ingredients in this chapter and—pow!—you've got yourself an entrée. Quinoa also works well during awards-season pun parties since it's "Joaquin" with swapped syllables. In my house on awards show evenings, we have pot-luck parties and everybody has to bring a dish named after one of the nominees. Say "quinoa" three times in a row. Are you saying "Quinoa" or "Joaquin"? When's Quinoaquin Phoenix's next nomination?!?!

Shrimp Quinoa (Chinese)

Shrimp Quinoa (Chinese)

PREP TIME: 12 MINUTES   /   TOTAL TIME: 45 MINUTES   /   SERVINGS: 6

....

2 c chicken broth (you can use veggie if you're dealing with anti-poultry people)

1 c quinoa

1 T olive oil

1 c oyster mushrooms, chopped

1 c enoki mushrooms

¼ lb. shrimp (about 6 large), peeled, cleaned, and chopped

1 c chopped baby corn (about 6 corns)

½ c chopped water chestnuts (about half a can)

3 scallions, chopped

1 T minced peeled fresh ginger

1 T chopped garlic (about 2 small cloves)

Salt and pepper

1½ T soy sauce (or tamari)

1 T sesame oil (chili sesame if you're feeling spicy)

....

Place the broth and quinoa in a pot, bring to a boil, cover, reduce the heat to low, and simmer for 12 minutes, until all of the broth has been absorbed. You can tell the quinoa is done when it looks fluffy, not swampy. (If you're using a small pot, you'll probably need to increase the cooking time by a few minutes.) Remove from the heat, fluff with a fork, and transfer to a mixing bowl.

Heat the olive oil in a skillet on medium-high heat. Add the oyster and enoki mushrooms and cook for about 3 minutes. Add the shrimp. Cook, stirring, for another 2 minutes. Add the baby corn, water chestnuts, scallions, ginger, and garlic, and season with salt and pepper. Continue sautéing until the mushrooms have released their juices and are beginning to brown, about 3 more minutes.

Add the pan contents to the bowl with the quinoa along with the soy sauce and sesame oil. Toss! Too-us! Too-us! Debate whether it's better than the food at your local Chinese place. (It is.)

WINE: **Rhône Blend**
PRODUCER: **Les Pallières 'Les Racines'**
REGION: **Gigondas, France**
Domaine Les Pallières is a winery in the Gigondas region of France's southern Rhône, where the wines bear some resemblance to Châteauneuf-du-Pape, but are slightly more affordable. It had formerly been run by the same family since Columbus sailed the ocean blue, the Spanish Inquisition, and everything else the 15th century provided. That was until the Brunier brothers of Vieux Télégraphe (our CDP pick see page 151) and importer Kermit Lynch bought it in 1998, hence taking it from Renaissance to renaissance. This is a Grenache-dominant blend, and its big fruit will pair well with the Chinese flavors of this dish without being too much to upstage the shrimp.

OPP: **Château de Saint Cosme, Domaine Santa Duc, Domaine du Grand Montmirail**

BAND: **Wilco**
ALBUM: *Sky Blue Sky*
YEAR/GENRE: **(2007), Alt Rock**
I'll admit it, I was really after the "Thanks I Get" bonus track, but wound up loving the whole album. And this unique take on a winter dish deserves a less obvious choice than "Yankee Tango Foxtrot." While "Please Be Patient with Me" may be one of my quieter theme songs, it's all about the triple guitar threat of "Impossible Germany" that never fails to get a live audience whooping at its climax. Whenever Wilco plays The Greek in L.A, there's a high chance I'll be ogling over their endless supply of bathroom stalls in the ladies' room. Best venue evs, and that's a multifactorially won award. It also never gets old hearing Tweedy serenade us with "California Stars" on home turf.

Ramps Quinoa (Italian)

PREP TIME: 12 MINUTES / TOTAL TIME: 45 MINUTES / SERVINGS: 6

WINE: *Vermentino*
PRODUCER: **Vigne Surrau 'Branu'**
REGION: **Sardinia, Italy**
Vermentino has many personalities depending on where it's grown, but on the Italian island of Sardinia, you're never far from the ocean! That proximity to the water gives an incredible salinity to the wine that results in an insatiable length on the palate. The bright green notes paired with the ramps and pancetta just scream Italian spring to me. This is another one owed to Matt.* Vigne Surrau exemplifies the melding of tradition and innovation in a winery. Their winery is state of the art yet created to blend in with the natural surroundings of the island.

*Other wines from Matt: see pages 135, 147, 163, 164 & 168

OPP: **Argiolas, Siddura, Capichera**

BAND: **Billy Joel**
ALBUM: *The Stranger*
YEAR/GENRE: **(1977), Rock**
"Scenes from an Italian Restaurant" and in this case we're going with a bottle of white over a bottle of red. We had the 8-track to *The Stranger* and it was tirelessly played in our green 1979 Cadillac Sedan DeVille. It's still just as good to this day. Fun fact: The 8-track had the songs in a different order than the vinyl or cassette. This is also up there with *Tapestry* for surefire sing-along, with other classics like "Movin' Out," "Vienna," and "Only the Good Die Young." When it comes to this quinoa dish, however, there won't be any leftovers for Brenda and Eddie.

2 c chicken broth (you can use veggie if you're dealing with anti-poultry people)	1 bunch fresh ramps (a.k.a. wild leeks), chopped (about ½ c)	¼ t red pepper flakes
1 c quinoa	½ c finely chopped pancetta	¼ c grated Parmesan cheese (or pecorino)
1 T olive oil	**Salt and pepper**	1 T lemon juice

Place the broth and quinoa in a pot, bring to a boil, cover, reduce the heat to low, and simmer for 12 minutes, until all of the broth has been absorbed. You can tell the quinoa is done when it looks fluffy, not swampy. (If you're using a small pot, you'll probably need to increase the cooking time by a few minutes.) Remove from the heat, fluff with a fork, and transfer to a mixing bowl.

Heat the olive oil in a skillet on medium-high heat. Add the ramps and pancetta and sauté until soft, about 10 minutes. Season with salt, pepper, and the red pepper flakes.

Add the pan contents to the bowl with the quinoa along with the Parmesan and lemon juice. Toss! Too-us! Too-us! So long, carbonara guilt.

CHEF'S LAGNIAPPE LESSON: Because pecorino is made from sheep's milk, it has lower lactose levels than Parmesan, which is made from cow's milk. I know a handful of people who can consume sheep and goat dairy with far less stress than cow.

"A bottle of red, a bottle of white
It all depends upon your appetite
I'll meet you any time you want
In our Italian Restaurant"
— *Billy Joel "Scenes From an Italian Restaurant"*

WINE: **Assyrtiko**
PRODUCER: **Gaia 'Wild Ferment'**
REGION: **Santorini, Greece**
We are really embracing the Mediterranean here. This green and flinty white comes from the Assyrtiko grape indigenous to the Greek island of Santorini. If I ever manage to get married, I dream of having a Greek summer wedding and serving this wine. Texture and body are more present than usual in this Assyrtiko due to twelve hours of skin contact. This is a variation from most Assyrtikos, which don't see any skin contact. The wine is then put into both oak and acacia wood barrels. The wild yeast strains take over at this point, and each barrel creates its own unique characteristics. You'll be "Dreaming" of competing with your guests to see who can drink whom "Under the Table" with this one.

OPP: **Hatzidakis, Domaine Sigalas, Boutari**

BAND: **Dave Matthews Band**
ALBUM: ***Under the Table and Dreaming***
YEAR/GENRE: **(1994), Rock, Jam**
The Greek wine pairing from my dad is a "Jimi Thing" and the music pairing is a "Jordan Thing." This album still holds up today—and I sing along to it like my 16-year-old self once did. I'll never forget working the Headcount booth at The Staples Center for a DMB show on the day when their original horn player LeRoi Moore, who was off the road because of some health issues, died. The halls were buzzing with the news before the doors opened. There wasn't a dry eye in the whole room. The band played their hearts out for him that night.

Chicken Quinoa (Mediterranean)

PREP TIME: 1 HOUR / TOTAL TIME: 2 HOURS / SERVINGS: 6

....

1 T tahini	**1 c quinoa**	¼ c chopped fresh parsley
¼ c plus 1 T olive oil	2 Persian cucumbers, chopped (about 1 c)	1 T chopped fresh oregano
¼ c lemon juice	1 c chopped tomatoes, lightly salted	**Salt and pepper**
1 boneless, skinless chicken breast, pounded thin	½ c crumbled feta cheese	
2 c chicken broth		

....

In a small bowl, mix the tahini, ¼ cup olive oil, and the lemon juice. Place the chicken breast in a resealable plastic bag and add half of this pasty mixture. Let it all sit to marinate for at least an hour in the fridge.

Place the broth and quinoa in a pot, bring to a boil, cover, reduce the heat to low, and simmer for 12 minutes, until all of the broth has been absorbed. You can tell the quinoa is done when it looks fluffy, not swampy. (If you're using a small pot, you'll probably need to increase the cooking time by a few minutes.) Remove from the heat, fluff with a fork, and transfer to a mixing bowl. Add the cucumbers, tomatoes, feta, parsley, and oregano, and season with salt and pepper.

Heat a grill pan on medium-high. Remove the chicken breast from the marinade, place on the grill pan, and grill for about 6 minutes on each side, until cooked through. (Don't overcook it—do you want it dry or do you want it juicy?) Transfer the chicken to a cutting board, let rest for 5 minutes, and then chop and coat with the remaining tahini marinade. (Don't use the marinade from the plastic bag unless you have a salmonella hankering.) Add the chicken to the quinoa and too-us! Come back from your momentary teleport to the Cyclades.

Chicken Quinoa
(Mediterranean)

Tofu Quinoa (Indian)

PREP TIME: 20 MINUTES / TOTAL TIME: 1 HOUR / SERVINGS: 6

WINE: Gewürztraminer
PRODUCER: Halleck
REGION: Russian River Valley, Sonoma Valley, California

On a recent trip to Sonoma, my friend Dana and I were hosted by Ross Haskell. I told him about this book, and he immediately knew his Gewürz was the answer to this dish, as it's almost exactly what he serves it with himself! Gewürztraminer is one of the most aromatic grapes, with notes of ginger, lychee, and spice. Because of this distinctive strength, it's often paired with Asian, Indian, and other flavor-forward cuisines. Ross's dog, Frankie, is a Basenji, which is the breed of Hula's first friend with whom she shared a crate when I found her. So she was thrilled to play with Frankie on our visit and help him keep the turkeys away from the famed Gewürztraminer vines.

OPP: Stony Hill, Navarro, Castello di Amorosa

BAND: Chris Robinson and Rich Robinson
ALBUM: Brothers of a Feather: Live at the Roxy
YEAR/GENRE: (2007), Rock

These two are right up there with the Oasis Gallagher brothers for on-again, off-again rock feuds (I hear it's really ovs this time but the optimist and dreamer in me refuses to accept it.) The Black Crowes founding brothers, Chris and Rich Robinson, performed this mostly acoustic string of shows. I was wise enough to catch one of the three L.A. shows and then flew to see it in NYC it was so moving. It was the only time I had been to The Roxy (hellhole) where they had seats on the floor. I was in a chair in the third row on Rich's side (duh) sandwiched between two girlfriends, completely entranced for two hours. Chills, tears. I laughed, I cried, it was better than Cats.

½ lb. extra-firm tofu (½ package)

SWOOPS

1 t ground cumin

½ t curry powder

1 T olive oil

2 c chicken broth (you can use veggie if you're dealing with anti-poultry people)

1 c quinoa

¾ c full-fat plain yogurt

½ c dried apricots, finely chopped

¼ c dried cranberries, finely chopped

¼ c toasted cashews, finely chopped

¼ t paprika

¼ t cayenne pepper

Drain the tofu by wrapping it in paper towels and pressing it with a weight such as the spare brick you probably have hanging out in your kitchen. An alternate idea for a weight is any container of liquid with a flat side, like a carton of milk. (You don't have boxed wine, so don't use that.) Let it hang out like that for 5 to 10 minutes. Once a bunch of liquid has drained, unwrap the tofu, finely chop, and place it in a bowl. SWOOPS. Add the cumin and curry powder. Too-us!

In a skillet over medium-high, heat the olive oil. Add the seasoned tofu and sauté for about 4 minutes, until slightly browned. Set aside.

Place the broth and quinoa in a pot, bring to a boil, cover, reduce the heat to low, and simmer for 12 minutes, until all of the broth has been absorbed. You can tell the quinoa is done when it looks fluffy, not swampy. (If you're using a small pot, you'll probably need to increase the cooking time by a few minutes.) Remove from the heat, fluff with a fork, and transfer to a large mixing bowl.

Add the tofu, yogurt, dried fruit, cashews, paprika, and cayenne to the quinoa and mix until fully incorporated. Say "Chalo" to anyone who tries to eat your portion. It means "Go away!" in Hindi, and it's one of three words I retained from our Zucker trip there in 2008. (At least this is what our tour guide told us we were saying; for all I know I could have been spewing profanities, but it did the trick.)

"You bring the letters and I'll bring the wine
And we'll keep on looking until the right time
For me to be better, so please be patient
'Til I see the world through the eyes of you"
— *Rich Robinson "Forgiven Song"*

SIDES
&
SAUCES

LEMON-DILL VEGGIES

This dish originated with the spring version, the apio (celery root) that was my Sephardic grandma's signature dish. Her name was Gracie, and she was the cutest. Her memorial in 2011 was a celebration of life. My mom, dad, and I all took turns telling our favorite Gracie stories and doing our favorite impressions of her Bulgarian accent. We almost took that show on the road. Her signature apio is now a staple at our Passover Seders, but the technique works well with many different vegetable bases. I remember her singing "Cielito Lindo" as she made it—you know, the mariachi song that goes "Ay ay ay ay, Canta y no llores!" (Spanish for "Ay ay ay ay, Sing and don't cry!") You'll be singing and not crying any day you dive into these recipes per Gracie's instruction.

Lemon-Dill
Beets

Lemon-Dill Beets

PREP TIME: 30 MINUTES / TOTAL TIME: 1 HOUR / SERVINGS: 8

6 medium beets, stems and greens removed

1 bunch dill, chopped (about ½ c)

3 lemons, juiced (about ½ c)

½ c olive oil

1 t salt

½ t pepper

In a large pot, bring enough water to a boil to fully cover the beets. Add the beets to the pot and cook for about 30 minutes, until a knife can easily cut all the way through them. Drain the beets, reserving 1 cup of the cooking water, then run them under cold water and peel them. The skins should slide right off. This would be a great opportunity to reserve two of the beets for a cocktail (see page 195). Slice the rest of them into ¼-inch disks and throw into a bowl. Add the dill, lemon juice, olive oil, salt, and pepper and too-us! Refrigerate for about an hour before serving cold.

WINE: **Portuguese White Blend**
PRODUCER: **Cartuxa 'Évora Branco' Colheita**
REGION: **Alentejo, Portugal**
Cartuxa shows us how close to Burgundy a white wine from Alentejo, Portugal, can come! With elegant power, blending Antão Vaz, Arinto, and Roupeiro grapes with a kiss of oak might fool a Master Sommelier into believing the wine was from one of the most famous Chardonnay appellations on the planet (Burgundy). Cartuxa takes its name from the Carthusian Monks who have lived in solitude and prayer in the monastery of Scala Coela since 1598 and started these vine plantings. The pairing here is on point. This winery's granitic soil lends to the crunchy and linear acidity and body that one would expect from a pretty white Burgundy. The earthiness and granularity of the beets actually get softened and tempered by the minerality of this wine. Thank Matt* for this one too.

*Other wines from Matt: see pages 135, 138, 163, 164 & 168

OPP: **Esporão, Mouchão, Cortes de Cima**

BAND: **Houndmouth**
ALBUM: *Little Neon Limelight*
YEAR/GENRE: **(2015), Alt Rock**
I was late to the game on this one but I've made up for lost time. With a seamless blend of folk, rock, and indie, you'll have it on repeat in no time. If you haven't heard "Sedona," do yourself a favor and hit Play on it immediately and you'll know why their music is so infectious and why I now talk about a "Saturday night kind of pink" when describing rosé wine, beet juice, or a particular lip gloss shade. I've been accused of making out with my dog. (Calm down. It's really more of a jowl smush than a *There's Something About Mary* outtake.) Here's another houndmouth I'm willing to kiss.

WINE: *Riesling*
PRODUCER: **Ronco del Gelso 'Schulz'**
REGION: **Friuli-Venezia Giulia, Italy**
I usually handle a Riesling better if it's bone dry like this one that our buddy Lou* blessed me with. It is big enough to match the acid of the lemon yet still tastes bright like the spring. The climate of Isonzo DOC in Friuli-Venezia Giulia bears the good fortune of both continental and coastal climates. The latter's warmer influence will create a more luscious, firmly structured white wine that balances out the high acidity of this dish. Two sips and "all trouble slowly fades away...through fields of joy."

*Other wines from Lou; see pages 68 & 80

OPP: Mitja Sirk, Element, Knebel

BAND: Lenny Kravitz
ALBUM: *Mama Said*
YEAR/GENRE: (1991), Rock
Mama said to eat your veggies! With his *Let Love Rule* debut two years earlier, expectations were high for Lenny's sophomore album. Once again delivering his patented combo of rock and R&B, the album did not disappoint and he quickly got a whole lot of offers to open for legends like Tom Petty and Bob Dylan. Also, you can safely munch double servings of this low-cal dish/wine/music combo and do all the rocker power squats freely without risking ripping your pants. Fun fact: My favorite UPenn a capella group Penn 6 did a mean rendition of "Fields of Joy" that turned me on to this album!

Lemon-Dill Celery Root

PREP TIME: 15 MINUTES / TOTAL TIME: 30 MINUTES / SERVINGS: 8

3 celery root knobs (a.k.a. apio or celeriac), peeled and sliced into ¼-inch disks

1 c chopped baby carrots (½-inch pieces)

1 bunch dill, chopped (about ½ cup)

3 lemons, juiced (about ½ c)

½ c olive oil

1 t salt

½ t pepper

Put the sliced celery root and carrots in a large pot. Cover with cold water and cook on medium heat until tender, about 15 minutes. Drain and transfer to a large bowl. Add the dill, lemon juice, olive oil, salt, and pepper and too-us! Refrigerate for about an hour before serving cold. Gracie always ordered "dee best deesh." Now you're serving dee best deesh.

CHEF'S LAGNIAPPE LESSON: Always bring food, such as a lemon-dill veggie, to your friends if they're in the hospital. Or else you risk them pulling "a Gracie." Like that time she called for the nurse and said, "Nehrse! Breeng me dee chef! Dee fud here hez NUH TEST!" (Nurse! Bring me the chef! The food here has NO TASTE!")

Lemon-Dill
Celery Root

WINE: *Sauvignon Blanc*
PRODUCER: **Cordon**
REGION: **Santa Barbara, CA**

We are finally diving into domestic Sauvignon Blancs—I can't believe it took until page 150. This one hails from Santa Barbara, and it's grassy and green and everything in between. The little slap in the face you get from the bite will keep you on your toes in the summer heat while the delicious fruit will keep you happy. Cordon prides itself on emulating the style of Sancerre, which leans on its chalky soil to impart flinty flavors, strong minerality, and lower alcohol as opposed to the fruitier, more herbaceous approach more common in New World Sauv Blanc.

OPP: Arrow & Branch, Gainey, St. Suprey, Prisma

BAND: Crosby, Stills, Nash & Young
ALBUM: *So Far*
YEAR/GENRE: (1974), Classic Rock

How many bands can compile a "greatest hits" record after only releasing two albums? In 1970, CSNY, the Grateful Dead, and Jefferson Airplane were all recording albums at the same studio at the same time in the Bay Area. In exchange for CSNY helping the Dead learn how to vocally harmonize better, Jerry Garcia laid down the pedal steel for "Teach Your Children." And that's Joni Mitchell's artistic skill featured on this album's front cover (along with her own albums). I took the alliteration lead from the "Helplessly Hoping" track and paired CSNY *So Far* with some sweet summer corn. I feel like harmony would be the forbidden word for the CSNY clue in Taboo.

Lemon-Dill Sweet Summer Corn

PREP TIME: 15 MINUTES / TOTAL TIME: 30 MINUTES / SERVINGS: 8

....

6 ears corn, husks removed

1 bunch dill, chopped (about ½ c)

1 lemon, juiced (about ¼ c)

½ c olive oil

1 t salt

½ t pepper

....

In a large pot, bring enough water to a boil to fully cover the corn. Add the corn to the pot and boil for about a minute. Drain and rinse with cold water. Cut the kernels off the cobs and place in a bowl. Add the dill, lemon juice, olive oil, salt, and pepper and too-us! Refrigerate for about an hour before serving cold.

CHEF'S LAGNIAPPE LESSON: Gracie's nickname for me when I was a baby was Shula Mamoola. Apparently "mamoola" meant corn in one of the various languages she had stored in her head (though I'm struggling to find confirmation of this "tale" on the Internet).

WINTER   SPRING   SUMMER   FALL

Lemon-Dill Cauliflower

PREP TIME: 15 MINUTES / TOTAL TIME: 35 MINUTES / SERVINGS: 8

2 heads cauliflower, stems removed, cut into small florets

1 bunch dill, chopped (about ½ c)

2 lemons, juiced (about 2/3 c)

½ c olive oil

1 t salt

½ t pepper

In a large pot, bring enough water to a boil to cover the cauliflower. Add the cauliflower to the pot and cook for 5 to 6 minutes, until tender. Drain and transfer to a bowl. Add the dill, lemon juice, olive oil, salt, and pepper and too-us! Refrigerate for about an hour before serving cold. What can't cauliflower do?!?!

WINE: **Southern Rhône Blend**
PRODUCER: **Vieux Télégraphe**
REGION: **Châteauneuf-du-Pape, France**
Most people pair cauliflower with a classic Bordeaux or a Burgundy. I dreamed a dream I was different and matched with a CDP. Châteauneuf-du-Pape (CDP) is the most famous region of the southern Rhône, where Grenache is the principal red grape. It is often blended with Mourvèdre and Syrah, but 18 different varieties in total are actually allowed to be blended into CDP, a leniency within France's otherwise strict guidelines. CDP is famous for its galets roulés stones, creating great drainage which forces the vines to have deep roots, making the wines powerful and structured. This is the absolute most accoladed and world-renowned Châteauneuf-du-Pape, with a remarkable combination of full fruit, elegance, and freshness.

OPP: **Château de Beaucastel, Domaine du Pegau, Château Rayas**

BAND: **Original Broadway Cast**
ALBUM: ***Les Misérables—Soundtrack***
YEAR/GENRE: **(1985), Show Tunes**
Drink with me! Sip some CDP and belt out these powerhouse show tunes revisiting the French Revolution. Based on the 1862 novel of the same name by French poet and novelist Victor Hugo—it took him 17 years to complete it following another of his books, *The Hunchback of Notre Dame*—it wasn't adapted for the stage until 1980 with music by Claude-Michel Shönberg. I saw it a few times on Broadway and countless times in our bunk doing nightly reenactments at camp. "A little fall of rain" will make the cauliflowers grow. You'll be the "master of the house" when you serve this combo.

"Teach your children well
Their father's hell did slowly go by
And feed them on your dreams
The one they pick's, the one you'll know by"
— *Crosby, Stills & Nash "Teach Your Children"*

GINGER-GARLIC VEGGIES

My mom and I are required to make our ginger-garlic Brussels sprouts at every Thanks-g dins (you're being bombarded with Zuckerisms right now). My dad knows his job is to peel the leaves, which apparently he feels is best achieved in his tighty-whities. He takes great pride in his work—and also complains about the tediousness of his task the whole way through. Cooking the sprouts wet enables them to steam and sauté simultaneously for a brighter color and softer consistency. Here are four versions of the simple yet studly Double G side, pants optional.

Ginger-Garlic Leafy Greens

PREP TIME: 8 MINUTES / TOTAL TIME: 15 MINUTES / SERVINGS: 6

....

1 bunch kale, ribs removed, leaves chopped	1 T olive oil	1 t soy sauce (or tamari)
	2 T chopped peeled fresh ginger	½ t salt
1 bunch chard (your choice: Swiss, red, rainbow, etc.), chopped	2 T chopped garlic (about 4 cloves)	¼ t pepper

....

Bring a large pot of water to a boil. Add the kale and chard and parboil in the water for 2 minutes. Drain. No need to plunge them into an ice bath because they're going straight to the skillet.

Heat the olive oil in a skillet on medium-high heat. Add the greens and sauté for about 5 minutes, until starting to wilt. Add the ginger, garlic, soy sauce, salt, and pepper and cook for another 5 minutes, tossing to evenly distribute all of the ingredients. Hits the GG spot.

WINE: **Grenache Blend**
PRODUCER: **Helmet Red**
REGION: **Santa Barbara, California**

This is a great table wine. The guys from Silverlake Wine stocked me up on it for my Girls Guide Chargers welcoming party, and there was not as much left over to take home as I'd hoped. It's an affordable California Grenache blend that tastes much pricier. In case L.A. decides to get yet a third NFL team, I'll be ready to welcome them with cases of this too. Helmet Red is fermented with native yeasts without any new oak. The absence of oak will help pair with a normally difficult set of leafy greens. We rebel against the misguided "classic pairing" of a big, over-oaked Napa Cab with creamed spinach seen in so many chain steakhouses. Buck the trend, Girls Guide style.

OPP: **Sine Qua Non, Pax Mahle, Whitcraft**

BAND: **Derek and the Dominos**
ALBUM: *Layla and Other Assorted Love Songs*
YEAR/GENRE: **(1970), Blues Rock**

Tell those leafy greens to "Keep on Growing." Eric Clapton holds special medium in the Zucker family as Betti and Jim's first date was at a Cream concert in the summer of '68. My mother lived across the street from one of my dad's fraternity brothers. Said neighbor asked her if she wanted to go see Cream. Thus arose my grandmother's infamous advice of "Go out weeth heem, you never knuh who hees friends are!" So my mom agreed and they were each to bring a friend. The rest is history. T or F: There is (or once was) a fully clothed picture of Eric Clapton in tight pants on the wall of the backstage room of the Hard Rock Café in Vegas that (seemingly) puts Ron Jeremy to shame.

WINTER SPRING SUMMER FALL

Ginger-Garlic
Brussels Sprouts

"I was laughing,
Playing in the streets, I was unknowing;
I didn't know my fate"
— *Derek and the Dominos "Keep on Growing"*

Ginger-Garlic Bok Choy

PREP TIME: 15 MINUTES / TOTAL TIME: 20 MINUTES / SERVINGS: 6

....

1 large head bok choy,
root end removed

1 T olive oil

2 T chopped peeled fresh ginger

2 T chopped garlic
(about 4 cloves)

1 T soy sauce (or tamari)

½ t salt

¼ t pepper

....

Chop the bok choy horizontally (parallel to root end cut) into 1-inch pieces. Rinse thoroughly in a colander, then shake to drain, but do not dry completely.

Heat the olive oil in a skillet on medium-high heat. Add the bok choy and cook for 5 minutes, until the greens start to cook down and the whites are slightly translucent. Add the ginger, garlic, soy sauce, salt, and pepper and cook for another 5 minutes, tossing to evenly distribute all of the ingredients. GG Whiz that was easy!

WINE: **Red Blend**
PRODUCER: **Fronton de Oro 'Malpaís'**
REGION: **Gran Canaria, Spain**
This wine is a blend of mostly Listán Negro and Tintilla grapes from the Canary Islands, a Spanish archipelago off the southwest coast of Morocco. Tintilla is another name for the Trousseau grape, which is often used for Port in Portugal. Give it a shot—it's a good bok choice! The natural spice of this red blend plays well with the ginger component of this veggie dish. Though it's difficult to grow grapes here—soils are poor, so vines don't yield a lot of fruit—the payoff is big. Bright red fruit intertwines with herbal, floral, and smoky notes, creating lots of layers to explore.

OPP: **Los Bermejos, Tajinaste, Envinate**

BAND: **R. L. Burnside**
ALBUM: *Come On In*
YEAR/GENRE: **(1998), Blues**
R.L. Burnside was born in rural Mississippi and is about as real-deal a bluesman as they come. Sharecropping, murder, juke joints...you name it, he's experienced it. It was largely through his work with the Fat Possum label in the '90s that he gained wider notoriety—this being the same label that would eventually break The Black Keys in the early 2000s (see page 114). One of his cohorts that he worked the juke joint circuit with, Junior Kimbrough, is another must-listen for fans of this hill-country blues. His last live performance was at Bonnaroo in 2004 with the North Mississippi Allstars before he passed away the following year.

Ginger-Garlic String Beans & Okra

PREP TIME: 8 MINUTES / TOTAL TIME: 15 MINUTES / SERVINGS: 6

....

1 T olive oil

1 lb. string beans, trimmed

1 lb. baby okra (you can use frozen if necessary)

2 T chopped peeled fresh ginger

2 T chopped garlic (about 4 cloves)

1 T soy sauce (or tamari)

½ t salt

¼ t pepper

....

Heat the olive oil in a skillet on medium-high heat. Add the string beans and okra and cook for 2 minutes, until just warm. Add the ginger, garlic, soy sauce, salt, and pepper and cook for another 5 minutes, tossing to evenly distribute all of the ingredients. Share your GG side, or someone might perform a little Gris Gris on you! (Gris Gris, pronounced "Gree Gree," is a form of Voodoo magic.)

WINTER   SPRING   SUMMER   FALL

Ginger-Garlic String
Beans & Okra

WINE: **Riesling**
PRODUCER: **J.J. Prüm**
REGION: **Mosel, Germany**
Even if you don't read German,
the country's wine labels are easy
enough to decode with a little
study. A German Riesling from the
Mosel region labeled trocken (dry)
and either QbA (Qualitätswein)
or Kabinett out of the QmP
(Prädikatswein) designations will
do quite well with these Brussels
sprouts. Remember to pass on
the other QmPs (Prädikatsweins):
Spätlese, Auslese, Beerenauslese,
and Trockenbeerenauslese.
Although often very good, you will
likely find them too sweet. The
Prüm family has lived in the Mosel
for at least 400 years, and they
were already famous by the 19th
century, so it's safe to say that J.J.
Prüm's Rieslings are top-notch.
Delicate body won't overwhelm
the veggies, but bright acidity will
stand up to that ginger bite.

OPP: **S.A. Prüm, Egon Müller,
Dr. Loosen**

BAND: **The Band**
ALBUM: *The Last Waltz*
YEAR/GENRE: **(1978), Rock**
I don't think I've met one person
who doesn't like this album. I
bet Martin Scorsese, who filmed
it all, would concur. Recorded
live at the Winterland Ballroom
on Thanksgiving Day, 1976. That
holiday, in my opinion, is all about
the sides and sauces. While
the original album is great with
appearances by Bob Dylan, Neil
Young, Van Morrison, and Joni
Mitchell, the deluxe edition nearly
doubles the songs to 40, including
a divine rendition of "Rag Mama
Rag" with Muddy Waters and
Pinetop Perkins. In an alternate
world, I return to the '70s and
make out with Rick Danko.

Ginger-Garlic Brussels Sprouts

PREP TIME: 15 MINUTES / TOTAL TIME: 20 MINUTES / SERVINGS: 6

1 lb. Brussels sprouts	2 T chopped peeled fresh ginger	½ t salt
1 T olive oil	2 T chopped garlic (about 4 cloves)	¼ t pepper

Cut off the root end of each sprout and peel off the green outer leaves until you're left with what looks like a little white and yellow cabbage head. Discard those little brainy-looking heads and keep the peeled leaves. Rinse the leaves in a colander; shake to drain, but do not completely dry them.

Heat the olive oil in a skillet on medium-high heat. Add the wet sprout leaves and cook for 1 to 2 minutes, until they turn an even brighter shade of green. (Be careful of the splatter.) Add the ginger, garlic, salt, and pepper and cook for another 4 minutes, tossing to evenly distribute all of the ingredients. Your Thanks-GG will never be the same.

CHEF'S LAGNIAPPE LESSON: Make your friend who claims to hate Brussels sprouts try these. The leaves are much more tender than the inner heads, and the generous seasoning of ginger and garlic will convert sprouts haters into lovers pretty effectively.

PESTO

Pesto is the best-o! It traditionally consists of basil, garlic, pine nuts, and Parm, but I found multiple green directions to take it in. Packing a punch with a concentration of herby flavor, it's multipurpose too, rendering this tasty paste a total kitchen all-star. You can use it to top pastas, eggs, veggies, meats, bruschetta, or to spike up your sando game. It's a super staple just to have on hand when you need to throw something together with the remains of the fridge. Eat your greens with zest-o!

Spinach, Parsley, Almond & Orange Pesto

PREP TIME: 5 MINUTES / TOTAL TIME: 10 MINUTES / SERVINGS: 8

¼ c raw almonds

1 c baby spinach

**1 c packed fresh parsley
(I like flat-leaf)**

**1½ t chopped garlic
(about 1 clove)**

½ t salt

¼ t pepper

**¾ c Parmesan cheese
(or pecorino; see page 138)**

1 T orange zest
(about ½ large orange)

1 t orange juice, freshly
squeezed (no store-bought
juice—you already have the
orange you zested!)

¾ c olive oil

Toast the almonds in a pan over medium heat until fragrant, about 5 minutes. (Check out the Spinach Salad recipes, pages 89 to 93, to learn what *not* to do in order to avoid burning your nuts.) Transfer them to a food processor and pulse until finely chopped. Add the spinach, parsley, garlic, salt, and pepper. Blend. Add the Parmesan. Blend. Add the orange zest and juice. Blend. While the processor is running, slowly drizzle in the olive oil. Scrape down the sides and finish blending until a smooth paste is formed. (Does anyone else have an irrational fear of the food processor blade?)

WINE: **Lambrusco**
PRODUCER: **Opera 02
"Amabile"**
REGION: **Modena, Emilia-
Romagna, Italy**
Lambrusco is such a little partier! It makes very famous "frizzante" wines (which are a little less sparkling than sparkling wines), but it's red! This almost-sparkling red wine is perfect for cold weather and food—especially something nutty or citrusy! I can always rely on Matt* to introduce me to interesting wines. Opera 02, much like pesto and Lambrusco, is extremely versatile. You can tour their vineyards, eat at their restaurant, or stay at their agroturismo. (All of the above, please!) Lambrusco pairs with a range of fatty and salty dishes. This is not your grandma's jug Lambrusco—this is going to be savory, dry, and delicious. "Amabile" means "lovely" in Italian and that's just how it'll make you feel.

*Other wines from Matt: see pages 135, 138, 147, 164 & 168

OPP: **Cleto Chiarli, Medici Ermete, Fiorini 'Becco Rosso'**

BAND: **Dr. Dre**
ALBUM: *2001*
YEAR/GENRE: **(2001), Hip-Hop**
Another hip-hop album I can stomach because it's really rooted in funk. The follow-up to his landmark 1992 debut *The Chronic*, *2001* once again proved Dre could rap *and* produce at a high level (pun intended). The album's Southern California, urban groove always gets my head bobbing with its funk-fueled beats and killer samples. I wonder if they told Snoop his call time was 4 hours before they needed him in the studio for his guest contribution. Has Dre ever sampled a food processor? Or "Also Sprach Zarathustra" (theme from Stanley Kubrick's *2001: A Space Odyssey*)? Things to ponder over pesto.

Mint, Lemon & Ricotta Pesto

PREP TIME: 35 MINUTES / TOTAL TIME: 45 MINUTES / SERVINGS: 8

½ c packed fresh parsley
(I like flat-leaf)

½ c fresh mint

1½ t chopped garlic
(about 1 clove)

½ t salt

¼ t pepper

½ c Parmesan cheese (or
pecorino; see 🐷 page 138)

½ c ricotta cheese

2 t lemon zest (1 lemon)

1 T lemon juice (about
½ lemon)

¼ c olive oil

Throw the parsley, mint, garlic, salt, and pepper into a food processor. Blend. Add the Parmesan and ricotta. Blend. Add the lemon zest and juice. Blend. While the processor is running, slowly drizzle in the olive oil. Scrape down the sides and finish blending until a smooth paste is formed. (Don't touch the food processor blade per your parents' firm childhood instructions.)

Oven-Roasted Tomato & Basil Pesto

PREP TIME: 35 MINUTES / TOTAL TIME: 3 HOURS 45 MINUTES / SERVINGS: 8

4 Roma tomatoes

SWOOPS

¼ cup pine nuts

1½ t chopped garlic
(about 1 clove)

½ c packed fresh parsley
(I like flat-leaf)

½ c fresh basil leaves

½ t salt

¼ t pepper

½ c Parmesan cheese
(or pecorino; see
page 138)

¼ c olive oil

Preheat the oven to 275°F.

Slice the tomatoes in half and place skin side down on a foil-lined baking sheet. SWOOPS and slow-roast in the oven until they're shriveled to half their original size, about 3 hours.

Toast the pine nuts in a pan over medium heat until fragrant, about 5 minutes. Transfer them to a food processor and pulse until finely chopped.

Add the tomatoes and garlic to the food processor. Blend. Add the parsley, basil, salt, and pepper. Blend. Add the Parmesan. Blend. While the processor is running, slowly drizzle in the olive oil. Scrape down the sides and finish blending until a smooth paste is formed. (Stare at the food processor blade and see if you can Jedi-mind-trick it to wash itself.)

WINE: **Nerello Mascalese**
PRODUCER: **Frank Cornelissen 'Contadino'**
REGION: **Sicily, Italy**
This is a chilled Italian red for the summer from Sicily, with a hint of fizz, a dash of funk, and a whole lot of fun. Made primarily with Nerello Mascalese, the key grape of the Etna region, this wine from producer Frank Cornelissen is a funky good time, there's nothing boring about it. The sweetness and umami complexities of the oven-roasted tomatoes appear to jive with a wine that seems to appeal to one's most primal desires. Frank Cornelissen is an eccentric, unwavering natural winemaker who is prouder of his failures than his successes. When you go to taste at his vineyard you are to taste his flawed wines before you get a glass of saleable wines. I always worked out my math problems in pen, so I'm naturally drawn to this philosophy.

OPP: **Girolamo Russo, Passopisciaro, Tenuta delle Terre Nere, Di Govanna**

BAND: **Talking Heads**
ALBUM: *Speaking in Tongues*
YEAR/GENRE: **(1983), New Wave**
After a bottle of Contadino I'm not sure what language I'm attempting. Italian? English? Doesn't matter—turn on some Talking Heads. You'll be speaking in tongues too. A group of art school punks from RISD (my best friend Andee's alma mater), this is the band's fourth album and first without producer Brian Eno. They split up in 1991 and played together in 2002 for their induction into the Rock and Roll Hall of Fame. We've been begging them to get back together ever since but instead David Byrne performed a solo "American Utopia" tour in 2018 as a "do we really need to" response.

WINE: Hondarrabi Zuri
PRODUCER: Bidaia Txakolina
REGION: Getariako, Basque Country, Spain

Txakoli (pronounced "cha-ko-lee") is a Basque wine that has captured the hearts and minds of white wine drinkers all over the world! Whether you've encountered it during your visit to the Guggenheim Museum in Bilbao, or were served it at one of the top restaurants in the world during your recent visit to San Sebastián, this often spritzy wine made from Hondarrabi Zuri (don't worry, no one can pronounce it correctly) packs a punch of flowers, citrus rind, orange oil, and seaside minerality! Matt* takes yet another bow for this one. Txakoli is traditionally poured with a very long pour to enhance that natural effervescence of the wine (think drinking from a porron—the original Spanish party decanter). I've found it on tap in a few tapas bars!

*Other wines from Matt: see pages 135, 138, 147, 163 & 164

OPP: Ameztoi, Txomin Etxaniz, Mokoroa

BAND: Fitz and The Tantrums
ALBUM: *Pickin' Up the Pieces*
YEAR/GENRE: (2010), Pop

If it's effervescent, quality pop that sparkles with soul like sunshine on water, look no further than this L.A.-bred band led by Michael Fitzpatrick. I've seen them at a bunch of my favorite L.A. venues — The Fonda, The Greek, and The Bowl — and it's always a good time. This album soundtracked a good portion of my summer hanging in 2011 with its dose of neo-soul and pop. Pop it in and dance while your pet will be Pickin' Up the Pieces of your pesto that dropped on the floor.

Pistachio, Tarragon & Lime Pesto

PREP TIME: 5 MINUTES / TOTAL TIME: 15 MINUTES / SERVINGS: 8

....

¼ c raw pistachios, shelled

½ c fresh tarragon

½ c packed fresh parsley (I like flat-leaf)

1½ t chopped garlic (about 1 clove)

½ t salt

¼ t pepper

¾ c Parmesan cheese (or pecorino; see 💀 page 138)

1 T lime zest (½ lime)

1 t lime juice (fresh from the ½ lime you just zested)

¾ c olive oil

....

Toast the pistachios in a pan over medium heat until fragrant, about 5 minutes. Transfer them to a food processor and pulse until finely chopped. Add the tarragon, parsley, garlic, salt, and pepper. Blend. Add the Parmesan. Blend. Add the lime zest and juice. Blend. While the processor is running, slowly drizzle in the olive oil. Scrape down the sides and finish blending until a smooth paste is formed. (Face your demons and bravely conquer washing that food processor blade.)

WINTER   SPRING   SUMMER   FALL

12-MINUTE TOMATO SAUCE

Unless you're a cute Italian grandma, you probably don't have the time or patience required for making a classic tomato sauce that sits on the stove and simmers for hours. Here's one that you can pound out on any given evening. The cherry tomatoes are a lower-acid variety so you can get away with the shorter cooking time. The base sauce alone will stand by itself, but the Zuckers like to spruce it up with extra flavors to give it a punch. The sauce is versatile; it will do well as a pasta sauce, spooned over fish, with eggs for breakfast, or slathered on crostini. I personally have no shame in just eating it with a spoon, much like the guac and steak sauces.

WINE: **Monastrell**
PRODUCER: **Bodegas Juan Gil 'Silver Label'**
REGION: **Jumilla, Spain**

Go big or go home! This is one of my favorite affordable wines, and it's a good match for the acidity in the sauce. This rich, powerful wine can stand up to both the acidity and sweetness of balsamic vinegar as well as the salty capers. At $12 a bottle, you'll think you've won the jackpot. Every sip feels more like $50. Monastrell is the Spanish version of the Mourvèdre grape, and this one is grown in Jumilla, in southeastern Spain. The Juan Gil winery is on its fourth generation of vineyard ownership and their focus has always been Monastrell. It should be no surprise that they are experts at creating Monastrell wines that taste way more expensive than they are.

OPP: **Bodegas El Nido, Clos Mogador, Torres**

BAND: **Lucius**
ALBUM: *Nudes*
YEAR/GENRE: **(2018), Acoustic Folk Pop**

I first fell spellbound to Jess Wolfe and Holly Laessig's harmonic voices during the Roger Waters set at Oldchella (name affectionately given to the Desert Trip festival due to its shared location with Coachella but attraction of slightly different generation). I was immediately captivated amidst the ultimate classic rock rager and jumped at the opportunity to see them perform at Largo, an under-the-radar local venue in my neighborhood that serves up anything but under-the-radar talent and surprises. While they do their cool indie folk thing with Lucius, these two have worked with a who's who of musicians, Jeff Tweedy, My Morning Jacket, Dawes to name a few. Like the Bodegas Monastrell, you won't believe its price tag. Put on some Lucius to slide into your winter meal.

Balsamic-Caper Tomato Sauce

PREP TIME: 8 MINUTES   /   TOTAL TIME: 20 MINUTES   /   SERVINGS: 8

....

¾ c olive oil

1 large yellow onion, chopped (about 1½ c)

Salt and pepper

2 pints tomatoes (cherry, grape, or vine), halved and lightly salted (see page 48)

2 garlic cloves, minced (about 1 T)

1 T minced anchovies

2 t capers

2 t balsamic vinegar

....

Heat the olive oil in a large skillet on medium-high heat. Add the onion, season with salt and pepper, and stir. Cook for 2 minutes. Add the tomatoes and cook for another 2 minutes. Cover and cook for an additional 5 minutes. Uncover and add the garlic, anchovies, capers, and vinegar. Stir and cook for another 3 minutes. Season with some more salt and pepper and taste your masterpiece. Total game changer, amirite?

Fava Bean Tomato Sauce

PREP TIME: 8 MINUTES / TOTAL TIME: 20 MINUTES / SERVINGS: 8

¾ c olive oil

1 large yellow onion, chopped (about 1½ c)

Salt and pepper

2 pints tomatoes (cherry, grape, or vine), halved and lightly salted (see  page 48)

2 garlic cloves, minced (about 1 T)

½ c shelled fresh fava beans

Heat the olive oil in a large skillet on medium-high heat. Add the onion, season with salt and pepper, and stir. Cook for 2 minutes. Add the tomatoes and cook for another 2 minutes. Cover and cook for an additional 5 minutes. Uncover and add the garlic and favas. Stir and cook for another 3 minutes. Season with some more salt and pepper and taste your masterpiece. Make a *Silence of the Lambs* fava bean reference.

CHEF'S LAGNIAPPE LESSON: To remove fava beans from their shells, place them in a pot of boiling water for 2 minutes. Drain, then pop the favas out of their casings.

WINE: **Pineau d'Aunis**
PRODUCER: **Julien Pineau 'Sucettes á l'Aunis'**
REGION: **Touraine, Loire Valley, France**
I quite possibly fell over upon tasting this wine at Marvin.* It's served cold, it's jammy, it's bright, and it tickles and pets you all at the same time. It's natural and induces spring awakenings with each sip. Thanks, Marvin! This one hails from the Touraine, on the southern bank of the Loire River. The winery is very new; Julien Pineau's first vintage was in 2015, after he took over this vineyard from a duo of now-retired Loire favorites. However, he uses many traditional vinification practices, like plowing his vineyards by horse. A short, whole cluster fermentation from 80-to 90-year-old vines captures the character of this inherently big variety while showcasing its light and fun side.

*Other wines from Marvin; see page 100

OPP: **Brendan Tracey, La Grapperie, Domaine de la Roche Bleue**

BAND: **The Meters**
ALBUM: *Live on the Queen Mary*
YEAR/GENRE: **(1975), Funk**
This was a live show on the *Queen Mary* riverboat hosted by Paul and Linda McCartney in the band's hometown of New Orleans. The announcer, Gary Owen, is my inner-thoughts voice-over man. This album isn't on Spotify yet, so after you've downed your Pineau, instead of drunk-dialing your ex, you can call your local congressperson, urging her to vote "yes" on this matter. I equate The Meters with New Orleans Jazzfest, so they're a solid lock for a spring dish. The Meters are the true godfathers of funk. They put New Orleans funk on the map, if you ask me. Why haven't they been inducted into the R&R HOF?!?!

PAIRINGS · WINE + MUSIC

WINE: **GSM**
PRODUCER: **Linne Calodo
'Sticks and Stones'**
REGION: **Paso Robles, CA**
Linne Calodo is my favorite winery in Paso, in the Willow Creek district. (It has my favorite tasting room architecture too.) The winery is named after the type of soils found in the region and refers to limestone and clay. Save room for dessert. If you want a full-throttle experience versus drinking a white, GSM (Grenache/Syrah/Mourvèdre) is often paired with caprese salad, which somewhat mirrors this sauce. This juicy, fruit-forward wine with soft tannins can hold up to the bold, creamy texture of mozzarella, yet will not overpower the delicate basil.

OPP: **Hearst Ranch, Torrin, Herman Story**

BAND: **Indigo Girls**
ALBUM: *Rites of Passage*
YEAR/GENRE: **(1992), Folk**
This album is the sonic equivalent of comfort food and guarantees that whoever is within earshot will sing along with you to (at least) "Galileo" if not the whole album. You'll definitely be bringing up reincarnation (of this sauce) over a couple of glasses of this Linne Calodo. If you listen closely you can hear Jackson Browne and David Crosby singing backups, which makes you want to sing along even more. You can take the Emily part and I'll anchor the Amy line. Now, of course, I'll take new meaning when I get to the line "I think I'll write a boo-ooook." (How long till my spoon gets it right?)

Basil-Mozzarella Tomato Sauce

PREP TIME: 8 MINUTES / TOTAL TIME: 20 MINUTES / SERVINGS: 8

....

¾ c olive oil

1 large yellow onion, chopped (about 1½ c)

Salt and pepper

2 pints tomatoes (cherry, grape, or vine), halved and lightly salted (see 🍅 page 48)

2 garlic cloves, minced (about 1 T)

1 c fresh mozzarella cheese cubes (½ inch)

½ c chopped fresh basil

....

Heat the olive oil in a large skillet on medium-high heat. Add the onion, season with salt and pepper, and stir. Cook for 2 minutes. Add half of the tomatoes and cook for another 2 minutes. Cover and cook for an additional 5 minutes. Uncover, add the garlic, stir, and cook for another 3 minutes. Turn off the heat. Add the rest of the tomatoes, the mozzarella, and basil. Season with some more salt and pepper and taste your masterpiece. *Mangia* time!

Green Olive Tomato Sauce

Green Olive Tomato Sauce

PREP TIME: 8 MINUTES / TOTAL TIME: 20 MINUTES / SERVINGS: 8

¾ c olive oil

1 large yellow onion, chopped (about 1½ c)

Salt and pepper

2 pints tomatoes (cherry, grape, or vine), halved and lightly salted (see page 48)

2 garlic cloves, minced (about 1 T)

1 c chopped Sicilian green olives (I like Castelvetrano)

Heat the olive oil in a large skillet on medium-high heat. Add the onion, season with salt and pepper, and stir. Cook for 2 minutes. Add the tomatoes and cook for another 2 minutes. Cover and cook for an additional 5 minutes. Uncover, add the garlic and olives, stir, and cook for another 3 minutes. Transfer half of the sauce mixture to a food processor or blender and puree. Return to the chunky sauce in the skillet and mix together well. Season with some more salt and pepper and taste your masterpiece. That's *amore*.

WINE: *Nouveau Pinot Noir*
PRODUCER: **Scribe**
REGION: **Carneros, Sonoma Valley, CA**
Inspired by the Beaujolais Nouveau tradition, Scribe—a terroir-driven winery just east of downtown Sonoma—replaces the traditional Burgundian Gamay grape with their own Pinot Noir to create this delightful, unfiltered red. It's usually released in November, making it the perfect autumn go-to. In the same tradition as Beaujolais Nouveau, the wine undergoes whole-cluster carbonic maceration and will sell out every year. Carbonic maceration produces a very light and fruit-forward wine, which will allow the green olive of the dish to shine.

OPP: **Division, Cep, Lo-Fi**

BAND:
Creedence Clearwater Revival
ALBUM: ***Willy and the Poor Boys***
YEAR/GENRE: **(1969), Southern Rock**
John Fogerty sings some timeless classics and a worthy mention in the ever-quotable *The Big Lebowski*. Wouldn't hold much hope out for the tape deck... or the Creedence. It's hard to imagine a band doing this now, at this level, but CCR put out all three of these killer albums in 1969: *Bayou Country*, *Green River*, and *Willy and the Poor Boys*. Each album is less than 35 minutes so they're perfect for this quick and easy time-conscious sauce. Hopefully I'll have arrived at a title for my book as successfully as the band arrived at their name. (They originally were The Blue Velvets and The Golliwogs before landing at Creedence!) No other band captured the cool swampy sound of the South hailing from California, El Cerrito specifically, a city outside San Francisco where John Fogerty grew up.

DESSERTS
&
COCKTAILS

CRUMBLES (a.k.a. Crisps)

The Zuckers love crumbles. So many desserts are time-consuming and require lots of prepping and waiting. Desserts can be complicated and daunting. One of the trickiest steps I've encountered in the kitchen is caramelizing sugar, a ubiquitous step in many desserts. (A friend who clearly has my sanity in her interest has since gifted me a candy thermometer, but I digress.) These rustic beauties can be thrown together rather effortlessly, on a whim with little forethought, and zero caramelizing required. Yet they're so impressive that your guests will think you're such a meticulous planner. They're also a great way to incorporate fruit into dessert. Sneak that nutrition in when you can!

Sweet Potato, Chocolate & Ginger Crisp

PREP TIME: 15 MINUTES / TOTAL TIME: 45 MINUTES / SERVINGS: 12

1 (10-oz.) bag chocolate chips (ones that taste good straight from the bag)

2 sweet potatoes, peeled and cubed

1 T minced peeled fresh ginger

1½ t granulated tapioca

1 lemon, juiced and zested

¼ c granulated sugar

¾ c brown sugar

1½ c all-purpose flour

½ c almond flour

¼ t salt

1 t almond extract

1¾ sticks butter, frozen (cut into small pieces)

Preheat the oven to 375°F.

Add the chips, sweet potatoes, ginger, tapioca, and lemon juice and zest to a 9-by-12-inch baking pan and too-us! Evenly distribute the contents in the pan.

Place the sugars, flours, and salt in a food processor and pulse until well combined. Add the almond extract and half the butter and pulse about 10 times. Repeat with the rest of the butter until a clumpy dough forms. If the dough isn't clumping, add water a teaspoon at a time until it does. You could also try scolding the dough if it's misbehaving. It's usually quite responsive to a good reprimand. Super effective.

Scatter the clumped dough on top of the mixture in the baking pan. Bake on the center rack of the oven for 30 to 35 minutes. The crumb should be golden brown and the potatoes should be cooked through. Remove from the oven and let cool for about 15 minutes. Serve it up warm, cold, or à la mode!

CHEF'S LAGNIAPPE LESSON: Though almond flour is readily available at many markets these days, my mother likes to make it herself at home. If you're itching to try it, simply grind 1 cup whole raw almonds in a food processor until you achieve a flour-like consistency.

WINE: **Pinotage**
PRODUCER: **Lammershoek 'LAM'**
REGION: **Swartland, South Africa**

From the Swartland region on the western coast of South Africa, just north of Cape Town, Pinotage is an indigenous red grape made by crossing Pinot Noir and Cinsault. The flavor profile of Pinotage is raspberry, blackcurrant, smoke, and hints of spice. The vineyard is planted near a forest also known as Lammershoek (meaning lambs corner). This is where the ewes would take their lambs to seek cover away from the evils of the Lammervanger, which is Afrikaans, a native language of South Africa, for black eagle. (Disclaimer: Jim would like you to know he doesn't like Pinotage. Jordan would like you to know he hasn't tried this one but we believe him. #moreforme)

OPP: **Kanonkop, Simonsig, Lievland**

BAND: **Prince**
ALBUM: *1999*
YEAR/GENRE: **(1982), Funk Rock**

We all made it through Y2K, but "1999" and "Little Red Corvette" are truly timeless. Perfect album for the end of the night. While he's got the look and prefers starfish, coffee, maple syrup, and jam, this dessert is as tasty as Prince. A glorious stylistic romp showcasing the Purple One's awesome array of talents with plenty of sex, rock and roll, and food references, this double album was originally envisioned as a triple album which was later released as *Crystal Ball* more than a decade late though it contained none of these songs. Because that's Prince. The man can write a song in the span of a sneeze and smirking wink.

WINE: **Counoise**
PRODUCER: **The Valley Project**
REGION: **Santa Barbara, California**

The wine made from this lighter French red grape grown in California tastes like a Jolly Rancher to me. We stopped by the tasting room in Santa Barbara after catching a Tedeschi Trucks show at the Santa Barbara Bowl on a girls' weekend celebrating one of us getting married. I think that's code for a bachelorette party when you're north of 30. This variety is known most as a blending grape in Châteauneuf-du-Pape but ripens fully in Santa Barbara where it stands on its own with The Valley Project. The rhubarb in this crisp is the dominant pairing flavor with the Counoise. Candy on candy. Try it chilled!

OPP: **Sea Smoke, Epiphany Cellars, AM/FM**

BAND: **Duran Duran**
ALBUM: *Rio*
YEAR/GENRE: **(1982), Pop**

Nobody is going to be *hungry like the wolf* after this dessert! Sweet and easy, this album is all '80s synth and glammy rhythms. I sometimes picture myself in an '80s rom com double-fisted with cans of Aqua Net hairspray ready to do battle with the already badly-damaged hair of my girlfriends who need help with their makeover. I'm also pretty sure at least three of my friends' houses growing up had large portraits of a woman by that dude Patrick Nagel who illustrated this album cover. This wine, album, and recipe will grow you a proper spring crop of shoulder pads and big bangs. All the better to rock to.

Strawberry, Rhubarb & Coconut Crisp

PREP TIME: 10 MINUTES / TOTAL TIME: 40 MINUTES / SERVINGS: 12

....

1 c finely diced fresh coconut (the smaller the dice, the better)

12 oz. (1-pint carton) strawberries, stemmed and quartered (see page 48)

1½ c diced rhubarb

1½ t granulated tapioca

1 lemon, juiced and zested

¼ c granulated sugar

¾ c brown sugar

1½ c all-purpose flour

½ c almond flour (see page 177)

¼ t salt

1 t almond extract

1¾ sticks butter, frozen (cut into small pieces)

....

Preheat the oven to 375°F.

Add the coconut, strawberries, rhubarb, tapioca, lemon juice, and lemon zest to a 9-by-12-inch baking pan and too-us! Evenly distribute the contents in the pan.

Place the sugars, flours, and salt in a food processor and pulse until well combined. Add the almond extract and half the butter and pulse about 10 times. Repeat with the rest of the butter until a clumpy dough forms. If the dough isn't clumping, add water a teaspoon at a time until it does. You could also try giggling and charming the dough to get it to do what you want. Maybe it just wants a spring fling.

Scatter the clumped dough on top of the mixture in the baking pan. Bake on the center rack of the oven for 30 to 35 minutes. The crumb should be golden brown and the strawberries should be jammy (because that's how I like it). Remove from the oven and let cool for about 15 minutes. Serve it up warm, cold, or à la mode!

Strawberry, Rhubarb &
Coconut Crisp

WINE: **Sparkling Red**
PRODUCER: **Frank Family Vineyards 'Rouge'**
REGION: **Napa Valley, California**

We hit this one up on our most recent Napa visit (which landed us at Halleck). I happened to not be the designated driver and was quite exuberant over this one. Dana, who was just taking sips and carting my chatty, happy ass around, was equally impressed with it. The wine came home with us—it's a summer party in a bottle. It's a Carneros red sparkling wine made in the traditional method comprised of Pinot Noir, Petite Sirah, and Chardonnay with lavender, vanilla bean, and black cherry flavor. This trifecta of flavors is partying with the white chocolate, red raspberries, and blueberries of the crisp. Fireworks in a bottle from the third-oldest vineyard in Napa is a grand old way to celebrate the grand ol' flag and red, white, and blue.

OPP: **The Chook Sparkling Shiraz, Fiorini**

BAND: **The Jimi Hendrix Experience**
ALBUM: *Are You Experienced*
YEAR/GENRE: **(1967), Psychedelic Rock**

This is a stunning debut album from arguably the greatest rock guitarist. My folks got engaged in the Summer of '69. They threw their engagement party on Aug. 17, which happened to conflict with a little music festival you may have heard of called Woodstock. To this day their friends are bitter and gripe about how they had to miss the event because Betti and Jim got engaged (though the upside is no one took the brown acid). Crank up the best anthem shredder on your next Fourth of July party, deck yourself and your food in red, white, and blue, and give a toast to your friends that sacrificed something that day to spend it with you.

Red, White & Blue Crisp

PREP TIME: 15 MINUTES / TOTAL TIME: 45 MINUTES / SERVINGS: 12

1 (10-oz.) bag white chocolate chips (ones that taste good straight from the bag)

2 c (two ½-pint cartons) red raspberries (see 💀 page 48)

2 c (1-pint carton) blueberries

1½ t granulated tapioca

1 lemon, juiced and zested

¼ c granulated sugar

¾ c brown sugar

1½ c all-purpose flour

½ c almond flour (see 💀 page 177)

¼ t salt

1 t almond extract

1¾ sticks butter, frozen (cut into small pieces)

Preheat the oven to 375°F.

Add the chips, raspberries, blueberries, tapioca, and lemon juice and zest to a 9-by-12-inch baking pan and too-us! Evenly distribute the contents in the pan.

Place the sugars, flours, and salt in a food processor and pulse until well combined. Add the almond extract and half the butter and pulse about 10 times. Repeat with the rest of the butter until a clumpy dough forms. If the dough isn't clumping, add water a teaspoon at a time until it does. You could also try mocking the dough and shaming it into submission. Anthropomorphization is not crazy.

Scatter the clumped dough on top of the mixture in the baking pan. Bake on the center rack of the oven for 30 to 35 minutes. The crumb should be golden brown and the blueberries should have burst. Remove from the oven and let cool for about 15 minutes. Serve it up warm, cold, or à la mode!

Peanut Butter & Fig Jelly Crisp

Peanut Butter & Fig Jelly Crisp

PREP TIME: 10 MINUTES / TOTAL TIME: 40 MINUTES / SERVINGS: 12

1 (10-oz.) bag peanut butter chips (ones that taste good straight from the bag)

12 figs, sliced vertically in half

1½ t granulated tapioca

1 lemon, juiced and zested

¼ c granulated sugar

¾ c brown sugar

1½ c all-purpose flour

½ c almond flour (see page 177)

¼ t salt

1 t almond extract

1¾ sticks butter, frozen (cut into small pieces)

Preheat the oven to 375°F.

Add the chips, figs, tapioca, and lemon juice and zest to a 9-by-12-inch baking pan and too-us! Evenly distribute the contents in the pan.

Place the sugars, flours, and salt in a food processor and pulse until well combined. Add the almond extract and half the butter and pulse about 10 times. Repeat with the rest of the butter until a clumpy dough forms. If the dough isn't clumping, add water a teaspoon at a time until it does. You could also try passive-aggressively sighing and eye-rolling the dough until it understands what you want it to do. The more sarcasm the better.

Scatter the clumped dough on top of the mixture in the baking pan. Bake on the center rack of the oven for 30 to 35 minutes. The crumb should be golden brown and the figs should be gooey. Remove from the oven and let cool for about 15 minutes. Serve it up warm, cold, or à la mode!

WINE: **Syrah**
PRODUCER: **The Blending Lab**
REGION: **Paso Robles, CA**
This one, made in L.A. with grapes sourced from Paso Robles, puts the jelly in a PB&J. A blending lab is about as unique as a PB&J, but The Blending Lab is extremely innovative regarding its public interaction and marketing. You can go to The Blending Lab and make your own wine to bottle and take home. We equally fell in love with The Blending Lab's Grenache, but for pairing purposes the Syrah had the fall crisp cornered—and we all know who likes it jammy! (T or F: Once upon a time, my JDate handle was ilikeitjammy.)

OPP: **Justin, Epoch, Booker**

BAND: **Various Artists**
ALBUM: *Glee! Soundtrack Vol. 1*
YEAR/GENRE: **(2009), Show Tunes**
A trio of guilty pleasures! I definitely guest-starred on this show nine times in my dreams. (My dreams involve a much-improved singing voice as well...) It may have joined the graveyard of weekly entertainment from a phase that included "24" and "Lost," but it gets reruns in my kitchen regularly. Current favorite utensil mic is the whisk, which recently knocked out wooden spoon. Let's put on a show! Guard your PB&J dessert in the school cafeteria; the other kids will want to steal it from you even if you're not in Glee Club.

COOKIES

Here are four really simple and scrumptious cookie recipes. These cookies may look basic, but just because they aren't loaded with mounds of chunks doesn't mean they're lacking in flavor—subtlety has never been my strong suit. You can dip them in milk or coffee, decorate them during the holidays, or just nibble on them plain and pure. Cookies serve as a great apology, too. Whenever I accidentally upset someone, I always win them back over with a batch of homemade cookies.

Miso-Maple Cookie

Miso-Maple Cookie

PREP TIME: 15 MINUTES / TOTAL TIME: 30 MINUTES / MAKES ABOUT 20 COOKIES

....

2½ c all-purpose flour

1 t baking soda

½ t baking powder

½ t salt

1 c (2 sticks) softened butter, at room temp

¾ c granulated sugar

¾ c brown sugar

1 egg

¼ c miso shiro paste

2 T maple syrup

1 T full-fat plain Greek yogurt

....

Preheat the oven to 350°F.

In a medium bowl, stir together the flour, baking soda, baking powder, and salt. Set aside.

Using a stand mixer, cream together the butter and sugars until smooth. Beat in the egg, miso shiro, and maple syrup. Beat in the yogurt. Gradually beat in the dry ingredients.

Scoop out 1 heaping tablespoon of dough and place on a naked cookie sheet. Repeat with the remaining dough, about 2 inches apart, until about 2 cookie sheets are filled. Slightly flatten the top of each cookie. Bake for 12 minutes, or until slightly golden and crackling. Transfer the baking sheets to a wire rack and let cool. Are you still mad at me?

CHEF'S LAGNIAPPE LESSON: My mom and I found that there was enough fat in the cookies to prevent them from sticking to the baking sheets, so we didn't need to prep the sheets with spray or butter. But if your cookies are sticking, obviously spray the day away. Also, we don't use foil because it was heating too quickly and causing the bottoms of the cookies to burn. Sorry about the extra step in cleanup!

WINE: **Natural Red Blend**
PRODUCER: **Axel Prüfer Le Temps des Cerises 'Fou du Roi' (the Jester)**
REGION: **Languedoc, France**
This is a natural wine from Bar Brutal in Barcelona. I got to patronize them one buzzed, blurry night on my recent Spain trip. You can Russian roulette a bottle of wine there and survive each shot with joyous pleasure. The Brutal Wine Corporation is a joint venture between multiple producers across Europe. All of the producers bottle their own wine under the same label. Axel Prüfer is a figurehead of the natural wine movement. This Carignan/Grenache/Cinsault blend is one of only four wines that he makes, all of which are harvested late to promote optimal ripeness. The umami of miso brings out all the great qualities of the Carignan variety in particular—funky and with an aliveness of character. The pairing could be simplified to the basic note of fermented miso with naturally fermented grapes. Try it chilled!

OPP: **Mas Coutelou 'Flambadou,' Henri Milan 'Papillon Rouge,' Chantereves L'Intrus**

BAND: **Ella Fitzgerald and Louis Armstrong**
ALBUM: *Ella & Louis Christmas*
YEAR/GENRE: **(2016; music is from the '50s), Holiday Jazz**
Ella and Louis are so cute. The yin to her yang, the salty to her sweet, this album and cookie are all about balance. These duets, which span several albums, never get old, especially during the holidays when despite being Jewish we get in the Christmas spirit of cooking, eating, and drinking (complete with Santa hats). Jews like Xmas too, people. So get into that holiday spirit and cozy up with this pair.

Lemon-Orange Cookie

PREP TIME: 15 MINUTES / TOTAL TIME: 30 MINUTES / MAKES ABOUT 20 COOKIES

WINE: Late Harvest Dessert Wine
PRODUCER: Château d'Yquem
REGION: Sauternes, France
This wine comes from the Sauternes region, in the southern part of the Bordeaux area known as Graves. It is the finest sweet wine in the world, made from Sémillon Blanc only in years when there is enough botrytis, or noble rot, which gives the wines notes of orange blossom and honey. The grapes are left on the vine until shriveled and left with highly-concentrated sugar, and only the best ones are individually selected by hand. The estate was the only one to gain the Premier Cru Supérieur designation in the 1855 Classification of Bordeaux (and, it was Thomas Jefferson's favorite dessert wine). Château d'Yquem takes all of Sauternes' labor-intensive and nature-dependent esteem to the next level and is hands down the most prestigious Sauternes house in the world.

OPP: Château Guiraud, Château Suduiraut, Château Doisy Daëne

BAND: Cake
ALBUM: *Prolonging the Magic*
YEAR/GENRE: (1998), Alt Rock
I figured Cake belonged in the dessert chapter linguistically, but it had to be a hot dessert stylistically. They deliver an utterly unique brand of bone-dry rock that manages to swing like weirdo campfire songs sung by a group of gifted social outcasts. I like them in measured doses like dessert wine. Cake's music always feels slippery like this highly viscous wine oozing down your inner cheeks. A big part of the band's sound is lead singer John McCrea's flat-toned, highly syncopated, almost spoken-word singing. I was always surprised that this album title was never adopted by Viagra as a company slogan; but a song of theirs did wind up as the opening credits of the action spy dramedy *Chuck*.

2½ c all-purpose flour

1 t baking soda

½ t baking powder

½ t salt

1 c (2 sticks) softened butter, at room temp

¾ c granulated sugar

¾ c brown sugar

1 egg

1 t lemon extract

1 t lemon zest

1 t orange zest

1 t orange juice, freshly squeezed

1 T full-fat plain Greek yogurt

Preheat the oven to 350°F.

In a medium bowl, stir together the flour, baking soda, baking powder, and salt. Set aside.

Using a stand mixer, cream together the butter and sugars until smooth. Beat in the egg, lemon extract, lemon zest, and orange zest and juice. Beat in the yogurt. Gradually beat in the dry ingredients.

Scoop out 1 heaping tablespoon of dough and place on a naked cookie sheet. Repeat with the remaining dough, about 2 inches apart, until about 2 cookie sheets are filled (see 🍪 page 185). Slightly flatten the top of each cookie. Bake for 12 minutes, or until slightly golden and crackling. Transfer the baking sheets to a wire rack and let cool. What'd I do now?

WINTER SPRING SUMMER FALL

Lemon–Orange Cookie

Vanilla-Rose Cookie

PREP TIME: 15 MINUTES / TOTAL TIME: 30 MINUTES / MAKES ABOUT 20 COOKIES

....

2½ c all-purpose flour	1 c (2 sticks) softened butter, at room temp	1 egg
1 t baking soda	¾ c granulated sugar	1 t vanilla extract
½ t baking powder	¾ c brown sugar	1 t rose extract
½ t salt		1 T full-fat plain Greek yogurt

....

Preheat the oven to 350°F.

In a medium bowl, stir together the flour, baking soda, baking powder, and salt. Set aside.

Using a stand mixer, cream together the butter and sugars until smooth. Beat in the egg, vanilla, and rose extract. (You could add 1 teaspoon rose powder and/or petals if you have access to them.) Beat in the yogurt. Gradually beat in the dry ingredients.

Scoop out 1 heaping tablespoon of dough and place on a naked cookie sheet. Repeat with the remaining dough, about 2 inches apart, until about 2 cookie sheets are filled (see 🍪 page 185). Slightly flatten the top of each cookie. Bake for 12 minutes, or until slightly golden and crackling. Transfer the baking sheets to a wire rack and let cool. Remorseful Rose to the rescue.

Cinnamon Cookie

PREP TIME: 15 MINUTES / TOTAL TIME: 30 MINUTES / MAKES ABOUT 20 COOKIES

2½ c all-purpose flour

1 t baking soda

½ t baking powder

½ t salt

1 c (2 sticks) softened butter, at room temp

¾ c granulated sugar

¾ c brown sugar

1 egg

1 t vanilla extract

½ t cinnamon

½ t freshly grated nutmeg

1 T full-fat plain Greek yogurt

Preheat the oven to 350°F.

In a bowl, stir together the flour, baking soda, baking powder, and salt. Set aside.

Using a stand mixer, cream together the butter and sugars until smooth. Beat in the egg, vanilla, cinnamon, and nutmeg. Beat in the yogurt. Gradually beat in the dry ingredients.

Scoop out 1 heaping tablespoon of dough and place on a naked cookie sheet. Repeat with the remaining dough, about 2 inches apart, until about 2 cookie sheets are filled (see 💀 page 185). Slightly flatten the top of each cookie. Bake for 12 minutes, or until slightly golden and crackling. Transfer the baking sheets to a wire rack and let cool. The cinnamon seems sincerely sorry.

WINE: Ice Wine
PRODUCER: Inniskillin
REGION: Niagara Peninsula, Ontario, Canada
O Canada! The grapes used to make ice wine in Canada (and Germany) are frozen while still on the vine, before fermentation, so they are not affected by noble rot but by freezing temps. The grapes are pressed with frozen juices so they yield a smaller amount but sweeter wine. Inniskillin is the premier ice wine producer of Canada. Cinnamon added to anything makes it wintery and upgraded. Ice wine embodies a richness on the palate of fruit with an acid backbone, and you're going to want to use it to wash down a cinnamon cookie "As Big As Your Face." (track 9)

OPP: Wayne Gretsky Estates, Mission Hill, Peller Estates

BAND: Galactic
ALBUM: *Late for the Future*
YEAR/GENRE: (2000), Funk
A Galactic show is my happy place. While I should probably devote an entire book, or at least a chapter, to this band, I'll just say that this was the CD that I had to remember to take out of my old car Coche the '92 Subaru SVX when I traded it in for Oscar the '01 Nissan Pathfinder. This was the album used as the opening music to my scenes at actor's showcases. And this was the album they were promoting when I first met the band at my 25th b-day party at their show at HOB in 2000. Hot-n-fresh with a pinch of spice like this cookie, this album epitomizes the new-school NOLA funk like few others.

TEQUILA COCKTAILS

Tequila rocks is my go-to cocktail (my current fave, a.k.a. "tequila candy," is Casamigos Reposado). I never add any sweetener to my drink—hold the agave at all costs. I spend half my life bargaining with bartenders to make my drink sans simple syrup, despite their resistance to serving it "unbalanced." (This is but one example of my situational behavior, with a running theme of "adorable or embarrassing?".) Just try these my way—you might surprise yourself!

Heartbeet-garita

Heartbeet-garita

PREP TIME: 1 HOUR / TOTAL TIME: 1 HOUR 15 MINUTES / MAKES 4 DRINKS

2 small beets,
ends trimmed

2 limes, juiced

1 t salt

2 c top-shelf tequila
(life's too short)

Bring a pot of water to a boil and add the beets. Cook for 30 minutes, until a knife slides right through. Drain, reserving 1 cup of the beet cooking water. When the beets are cool enough to handle, peel off the skins and dice the beets.

In a blender, combine the diced beets and reserved beet water until smooth. Add the lime juice, salt, and tequila. Blend again until Smooth Criminal status achieved. (Annie's OK.)

Pour the drink into 4 glasses over ice (rocks). Garnishing options include a salt-rimmed glass—or cocoa if you don't have 100/60 blood pressure to strut—extra beet cubes skewered on a gay cocktail umbrella, or the good old-fashioned lime wedge.

CHEF'S LAGNIAPPE LESSON: For these cocktails, I encourage you to use the glass shape of your choice. I personally like old-fashioned glasses—short and stout. Martini glasses are the stilettos of barware to me: best looking and least practical. Being sexy hurts.

WINE: You lush, you already have a drink!

BAND: **Michael Jackson**
ALBUM: *Bad*
YEAR/GENRE: **(1987), Rock, Pop**
MJ = **D**ance Party ensues. Whether straight or a letter in LGBTQ, no one can deny the King of Pop. A few Heartbeets deep, you slip this on and your party suddenly starts moving and grooving thanks to the one-two punch of "Bad" and "The Way You Make Me Feel." Hee Hee Hee. Aaow! *Bad* is the third in a trifecta of perfection (*Off the Wall*, *Thriller*) thanks in no small part to the production of original badass mofo Quincy Jones, who turns out to have played a role in an insane number of musical careers. Look him up—he's the cat's pajamas and the bee's knees.

WINE: Is it "Beer before liquor, never sicker" or "Beer before liquor, drunk quicker"? Hopefully it's not "boyfriend bicker" or "fight picker." Hold your alcohol, people!

BAND: Huey Lewis and the News
ALBUM: *Sports*
YEAR/GENRE: **(1983), Pop Rock**
Huey Lewis has aged as gracefully as any rock star I can think of. Three albums in, Huey hits a grand slam with "The Heart of Rock & Roll," "Heart and Soul," "I Want a New Drug," and "If This Is It." It will surprise you how happy this album makes people—trust me. The tasty sax licks, easygoing synths and overwrought electric guitar deliver a guilt-free '80s delight thanks to Huey's R&B chops cutting through it all. Perfect spring impromptu party planner.

Kumquat-garita

PREP TIME: 10 MINUTES / TOTAL TIME: 15 MINUTES / MAKES 4 DRINKS

....

16 kumquats, rinsed, halved, and green knob ends trimmed

1 sweet lime, juiced

1 T chopped peeled fresh ginger

1 t sugar (I'm not a hypocrite—the kumquats are too tart without it!)

1 c top-shelf silver tequila, chilled

....

Muddle the kumquats, sweet lime juice, ginger, and sugar in a bowl. Divide the mixture among 4 glasses (see 🎭 page 195). Pour the chilled tequila on top. Give it a stir. Kumquat here often?

CHEF'S LAGNIAPPE LESSON: Watch Wes Anderson's movie *The Darjeeling Limited* if you're unfamiliar with this citrus. You'll forevermore be doing your best Owen Wilson impression whenever you say "sweet lime."

WINTER **SPRING** SUMMER FALL

"Heir" of the Dog-arita

PREP TIME: 4 HOURS / TOTAL TIME: 4 HOURS 15 MINUTES / MAKES 4 DRINKS

8 large heirloom tomatoes, halved vertically

SWOOPS

2 garlic cloves

2 large kosher dill pickles (the garlicky, salty kind, not the sugary or vinegary kind), chopped, plus ¼ c pickle juice from the jar

¾ c chopped fresh dill

½ c fresh lemon juice (about 2 lemons)

2 T grated fresh horseradish

2 fresh jalapeño chiles, chopped (about 2 T)

1 t salt

½ t pepper

1 c top-shelf silver tequila

Preheat the oven to 275°F.

Place the tomato halves skin side down on a foil-lined baking sheet. SWOOPS! SWOOPS the garlic cloves and throw them on the baking sheet as well. Put in the oven and slow-roast for about 4 hours, until the tomatoes are starting to shrivel. If the garlic starts to get too brown, you can give it an early exit from the oven. Let cool.

Put everything non-alcoholic (that's the tomatoes, garlic, pickles, pickle juice, dill, lemon juice, horseradish, jalapeños, salt, and pepper) in a blender and blend until smooth, about 1 minute. Add the tequila and blend until well combined. Pour into 4 glasses (see 🌀 page 195) over ice and adjust seasonings. Warn people that they won't be able to taste the 2 shots of tequila, so if they're getting schnockered, that's why.

WINE: Whine: Not enough wine pairings!

BAND: **Various Artists**
ALBUM: ***The Big Chill Soundtrack***
YEAR/GENRE: **(1983; music is from the '60s), Motown**
This is the touchstone movie for every baby boomer parent, Betti and Jim included. The soundtrack is all killer R&B save for Three Dog Night's "Joy to the World" and Procol Harum's "A Whiter Shade of Pale," which was mistaken for The Band by a guy during an adult sleepover. He didn't like that I was right and that was the end of that run. This movie always gives me an emotional hangover which for sure begs for heir of the dog.

"Heir" of the Dog-arita

PAIRINGS ° WINE + MUSIC °

WINE: Shmine.

BAND: **Wham!**
ALBUM: *Make It Big*
YEAR/GENRE: **(1984), Pop**

This is R&B pop perfection. I didn't realize when it first came out and took American radio by storm and I fell in love with it like every other tween, but now, having plenty of Bill Withers, Otis Redding, and Sam Cooke under my belt, it's freakishly clear that the only difference between it and '60s R&B is the '80s sound synths and effects throughout it. George Michael was too big a talent to be caged in this duo for more than three albums. Whoever can name the other guy in the band gets another Hot Pear-garita. Give up? Andrew Ridgeley. (I'll share my drink.)

Hot Pear-garita

PREP TIME: 10 MINUTES / TOTAL TIME: 15 MINUTES / MAKES 4 DRINKS

· ·

4 Bartlett pears, peeled, cored, and diced

1 fresh jalapeño chile, chopped (about 1 T)

1 t salt

1 c top-shelf silver tequila, chilled

6 finger limes (caviar limes), sections squeezed out

· ·

In a blender, puree the pears, jalapeño, salt, and tequila until smooth. I mean like glacier-ice smooth. Have you had a cocktail made with glacier ice? It's much denser than regular ice and yields a perfectly smooth cocktail. Since you're probably not traveling with this book to Alaska, just keep that blender going for an extra minute. Pour into 4 glasses (see page 195) and sprinkle the lime caviar on top (about 1 teaspoon for each glass). Mmmmm.

"Another vacation is over
A September morning
With the sun and the smell of the clover"
— *Wham! "Another Summer"*

ACKNOWLEDGMENTS:

I may give the impression that I'm my own one-woman show/one-man band/solo soldier, but as we all know, it takes a special forces army to just get the dog walked every morning. This book would never have happened without the attention, blood, sweat, and tears (due to hysterical giggle fits) of the following people:

My parents, Betti and Jim Zucker. These people not only influenced my kitchen, bar, and concert skills, but also my sense of humor, ability to think big, love life, and ambition to share it with the world. Thank you for thinking an A- was ok, but why the minus? Thank you for making me feel like I'm supposed to be over-achieving. And thank you for finding me hilarious since I was a child. Without that enabling encouragement I'd not know to persevere.

Alex/Amanda/Bertolet - Thank you, my fellow writer friends, for taking the time to edit both copy- and content-wise. The more eyes on the book the better. I value your judgements and opinions, and trust your impressive grasp of our English language. Cheers to you.

Andee - Your artistic eye and unwavering emotional support was instrumental to my life in general and the fruition of the book. I'm pretty sure this means you can fly on airplane with me for free if you sit in my lap and we put you in a vest!

Ari - Thank you for taking the time to teach me PowerPoint so I could better communicate with my book designer. I may have never actually used it after you showed me, but just knowing it was possible was great for my morale. You're a peach! (And not just during the summer with the Allman Brothers.)

Ben/Chris/Tom- The pre-press and proofreading all-star team! Thanks for anchoring the final stages of the book. The home stretch heroes FTW!

Courtney - You kicked ass editing the wines. Way to jump right in and grasp my voice as if you've been hearing me blabber on for years.

Dbo - Working with a friend can be a double-edged sword. After working with you on the illustrations for this book it just makes so much sense why we're friends. We speak the same language. You understand me. Or maybe you're just really good at your job. Regardless, you're responsible for making my book cute. Thanks.

Elizabeth - Thank you for teaching me that I can't use the word "blanche" unless there's an ice bath involved, and for confirming my stance on the whole acronym/initialism debate. For the record, dear readers, I'm of firm belief that an acronym must be pronounced as a word whereas initialism is pronounced by saying each individual letter, despite Merriam-Webster's tendency to go soft on incorporating common mistakes into our vernacular. For example, "ASAP"—the abbreviation for "as soon as possible"—is an *acronym* if you pronounce it "ey-sap," and an *initialism* if you pronounce it "ey-ess-ey-pee."

Jay - If you're reading this, then we did it! Thanks for taking on a first-timer and all of her questions.

Jill - Your interpretation of my wording could be rivaled by no other. If there's a mistake in this sentence, it's because I didn't want you to read it until it went to print. Thank you!

Josh - The music blurb hero! Thanks for jumping right in and efficiently and effectively harnessing my ideas and making sense of my pairings grid.

Laura - I don't think I could have found a more respectful and gracious editor. I stayed upright when I was feeling ledgy through this journey because I had you in my corner. Let's go "Chalo" all over the damn country together.

Myjah - Thank you for your wonderful wine knowledge! The pairings and my education level are off the chains due to your wealth of information. Let's drink some all over the world together soon.

Peter - Way to turn my house into a full-on photo shoot set and photograph the shit out of my recipes. And for safely placing Hula into an Uber when I needed her at a party. Let's do all of that again for no good reason!

Signé - Thanks for helping me realize my vision for this book. It was so dreamy to see it all come to life on the page. You're the champion of the book design marathon.

Susan - Thanks for being fast, efficient, and reliable. The Oxford comma and I appreciate it.

Vivian - You are a force of nature, a superstar, a true professional. The joy of witnessing you transform my recipes into visions of beauty was just a phenomenon. Vivian for prez.

"Five hundred twenty-five thousand six hundred minutes
How do you measure, measure a year
How about love
Measure in love
Seasons of love"
— *Jonathan Larson "Rent"*

INDEX:

"And I start to feel the fever
From the warm air through the screen
You come regular like seasons
Shadowing my dreams"
— *Indigo Girls "Ghost"*

ABOUT THE AUTHORS:

JORDAN ZUCKER is an accomplished writer, actor, host, cook, and entertainer. She likes to creatively incorporate meals into every type of celebration (and who can't find at least one reason to celebrate a day...). She has shared her expertise as a guest star on Food Network's *Grill It! with Bobby Flay,* and has entertained audiences as "Lisa the intern" on NBC's *Scrubs.* She continues to educate, engage, empower, and entertain through her own comedic sports series, *Girls Guide to Sports,* which she writes, hosts, and produces. She combined her love of football and food in her "Monday Night Matchup Menus" series, creating meals each week based on the teams playing on *Monday Night Football.* She has expanded into cooking for other sports on the Girls Guide website. Jordan was featured with her mother, Betti, in the November 2014 issue of the Stampington & Company magazine *Where Women Cook.* You can follow her adventures through the culinary, cocktail, and concert world in her *Oxtails, Cocktails, and Rock Tales* blog. Jordan attends live music concerts religiously and keeps abreast of current gems and classic legends in the music world. Here, she combines three of her biggest passions, food, wine, and music, to bring you her first book.

BETTI ZUCKER is an accomplished cook and all-around master in the kitchen. She learned from the best, taking cooking classes from renowned chefs John Clancy and Lydie Marshall. Betti then went on to assist Marshall in her cooking school and tested recipes for her cookbook *Passion for Potatoes.* Betti worked in the Macy's cooking school De Gustibus, where she assisted many chefs, including Alice Waters, Jacques Pépin, Wolfgang Puck, and Patricia Wells. She also taught at Long Island Adult Education and in private cooking classes. Her recipes have been published in Molly O'Neill's *New York Cookbook*, and she has appeared on a TV cooking segment on the Long Island Education Channel. She was featured in the November 2014 issue of *Where Women Cook* with Jordan in their Vermont home.

JIM ZUCKER likes his wine. And yes, that is why his vinegar is so good. Jim was exposed to the world of fine wine at the tender age of 18, when he became a sommelier for the Grace Line, a steamship company that operated passenger and freighter vessels between the U.S. and South America. He was soon establishing his own cellar of '66 and '70 Bordeaux. Expanding to Burgundies and Rhônes, he became active in the New York City wine scene and befriended Alexis Lichine. Contributing to Lichine's famous luncheon tasting of '78 white Burgundies and '82 first-growth Bordeaux, he infamously but correctly identified one Corton-Charlemagne entry as "an imposter, a *vin de médecin*" (a pejorative term literally meaning "doctored wine," or a wine made of lesser grapes than what the label claims). Traveling the world with his family, exposing his discerning palate and superb memory to the food and wine of various domains, he remains passionate about aroma, taste, and finish. He is the original Zucker raconteur.

HULA ZUCKER likes her wine too. A tiny-but-mighty, ripped French Bulldog, she's 8 years old, a Scorpio, and enjoys snorting on the couch and post-bath happy laps. She is like sunshine: People's faces light up as she walks by them on the street. Signature feature: tongue that hangs out to the left. Favorite song: "In the Summertime" by Mungo Jerry. Food nicknames: Marshmallow, Mashed Potato, Alfredo Meatball, White Chocolate Truffle Log, Chicken Nugget, Dumpling, Rice Pudding, and Walrus. She regularly attends dinner parties but often sleeps through cleanup. But she's an Olympic snuggler so she's allowed. Betti was so obsessed with her grandpuppy that she got a Frenchie for herself: a blue brindle she named Sesame. Like daughter, like mother.